The
Farscape
Episode Guide
for Season Two

An Unofficial,
Independent Guide
with Critiques

by
Talis Pelucir

Lightning Rod Limited
Port Orchard, Washington

The Farscape Episode Guide for Season Two
An Independent Unofficial Guide with Critiques
copyright 2000 and published by
Lightning Rod Limited

ISBN 1-883573-55-6
9 8 7 6 5 4 3
Cover by Buster Blue of Blue Artisans

Lightning Rod Limited is a division of Windstorm Creative Ltd., a six imprint, international organization involved in publishing books in all genres including electronic publications, producing games, toys, video and audio cassettes as well as producing theatre, film and visual arts events. The lightning bolt on the web logo is a trademark of Windstorm Creative Ltd.

Lightning Rod Limited
7419 Ebbert Drive Southeast
Port Orchard WA 98367
1 360 769 7174
farscape@arabyfair.com
www.arabyfair.com

Acknowledgements

Thanks to everyone at Lightning Rod,
especially Jenn and Cee for their
editorial input and Tony for
telling me to wait.

Dedication

To the cast, creative team and crew.
But especially, to Cee.

Author Biography

Talis Pelucir lives with his wife and young son
near Ullswater, England.

Other Titles by Talis Pelucir

The Farscape Episode Guide for Season One:
An Independent Unofficial Guide with Critiques
The Farscape Internet Guide
The X-Files Internet Guide
The Buffy the Vampire Slayer Internet Guide
The Star Wars Episode One Internet Guide
The Pokemon Internet Guide
The Gillian Anderson Episode Guide
The Sandra Bullock Internet Guide

The
Farscape
Episode Guide
for Season Two

An Unofficial,
Independent Guide
with Critiques

by
Talis Pelucir

Lightning Rod Limited
Port Orchard, Washington

Table of Contents

Preface   9

Mind the Baby   11

Vitas Mortis   16

Taking the Stone   20

Crackers Don't Matter   26

Picture if You Will   31

The Way We Weren't   35

Home on the Remains   44

Dream a Little Dream   53

Out of Their Minds   59

My Three Crichtons   64

Look at the Princess Part 1:
A Kiss is But a Kiss   67

Look at the Princess Part 2:
I Do, I Think   75

Look at the Princess Part 3:
The Maltese Crichton   84

Beware of Dog   93

Won't Get Fooled Again   98

The Locket   110

The Ugly Truth   116

A Clockwork Nebari   127

Liars, Guns and Money Part 1:
A Not So Simple Plan   136

Liars, Guns and Money Part 2:
With Friends Like These   143

Liars, Guns and Money Part 3:   152
          Plan B

    Die Me, Dichotomy   162

Preface
Regarding Critiques
and the Official Episode Guide

As you're reading my critiques, remember: **I really love this show**. The critiques are my personal opinion based on my background as an author and a teacher of literature and drama. So my "take" on the episodes is going to come from a storyteller's perspective, a literary perspective.

As a published writer, one of the first aspects of a TV show I look at is the plot. Have I read or seen this before? Where? If so, why have the writers chosen to use the same basic storyline here? What does it reveal about the characters? Where does it work? Where doesn't it?

Because I've read so much science fiction, fantasy and world mythology, I sometimes become impatient when writers on any particular show don't stretch their creative muscles enough to present us with something new. But I also understand that what they write as well as what is presented is governed not just by their own inspiration and understanding of the characters and show's premise, but also by viewer feedback via various media (including BBoards), advertising dollars, the producer's vision, the director's vision and more. The actors, like the writers, often don't have much control — if any — over what happens to the characters. Ratings are big business and big money and if a show wants to stay on the air, everyone involved will try to hit the largest demographic in order to keep it going.

This sometimes means that the premise of a particular episode, or in some cases a whole series, will be based on a formula of what has worked before. And that's okay. I understand how the industry works and luckily, Farscape doesn't often fall into these traps.

Lastly, let me say again that these critiques are only my opinions. You will certainly have your own. Sometimes you will agree with me and other times you won't. And that's exactly as it should be. This is one of the main reasons Lightning Rod Limited publishes unofficial critique guides — because they are full of honest opinions not influenced by the numerous pressures I mentioned earlier.

However, I do encourage all readers to purchase the Official Farscape Episode Guides because they will most likely offer behind-the-scenes or "insider" information that an unofficial guide cannot. Additionally, you can check out The Farscape Internet Guide which will lead you to the most unique Farscape websites on the Internet. You'll find a lot of different opinions of the episodes on the web as well as places you can share your own thoughts about the show.

Episode 10202: Mind the Baby
Location: An asteroid field in the Uncharted Territories
Guest Cast:
Lani John Tupu as Captain Bailar Crais
Wayne Pygram as Scorpius
David Franklin as Lt. Braca
Writer: Richard Manning
Director: Andrew Prowse

SYNOPSIS:

This first episode of Season 2 (numbered as episode 2), finds Moya's crew separated and Talyn (Moya's newborn offspring) under Captain Crais' command. In the time between "Family Ties" and the opening scenes of this episode, Aeryn has managed to elude the Peacekeeper prowlers and rescue John and D'Argo. She's taken them to a small relatively hospitable asteroid and has been searching for food and water to sustain them until D'Argo regains consciousness.

Moya, in the meantime, is crewed by Chiana, Rygel and Zhaan. When they're attacked by the Sheyang, Zhaan seems to have a break with reality and calls out to D'Argo to help them. She retreats to her quarters to meditate, leaving Chiana and Rygel to help Pilot find the others. Chiana and Rygel contemplate jumping ship, resulting in an ascerbic exchange with Pilot.

Soon after D'Argo awakens, we learn that Aeryn has made a secret deal with Crais. It seems that Crais is having some trouble controlling Talyn and he agrees to find a safe haven for Aeryn to hide her comrades in exchange for Aeryn's help with Talyn. Crichton and D'Argo suspect Aeryn isn't telling them the whole truth and when she reveals her deal with Crais, D'Argo gives her a tongue lashing that literally sends her into unconsciousness. Crichton goes after Crais.

Some time later, Crichton manages to capture Crais

and return him to Moya. Chiana, overjoyed to see John, leaps into his arms. Thus reunited, she takes him to see Zhaan, who behaves as though Crichton is dead, despite appearances to the contrary. Other problems, however, seem more insurmountable. Talyn, confused and troubled, will not respond to Aeryn, but demands to have Crais returned, believing Crais is his one true friend. As the Peacekeeper Command Carrier bears down on Moya once more, Aeryn decides that she will accompany Crais aboard Talyn in the hopes of comforting Talyn and eventually returning to Moya with or without Talyn and Crais.

Once aboard Talyn, however, the hybrid leviathan offers Crais "the hand of friendship" which is in essence a neural interface which will allow Crais to "pilot" Talyn without the use of a command center like the one found on Moya. Clearly devastated by Talyn's choice of companion and sent away by the newly-bonded Talyn and Crais, Aeryn returns to Moya, leaving them just enough time to try and outrun the Command Carrier once more.

CRITIQUE:

There is, unfortunately, not much that works in this episode. Much of the information is revealed in exposition rather than dramatized. The most powerful and noticeable example of this is the entire arrangement between Aeryn and Crais. What a provocative sequence that could have been as part of the Season 1 finale! Instead of wasting our their time with "Bone to Be Wild" (which was a fine episode, but did not belong in the season finale arc) the creative team could have actually filmed and shown the audience how the arrangement between Aeryn and Crais came to be, leaving us with the question of whether or not Aeryn was a traitor during the hiatus between Seasons 1 and 2. It's too bad the creative team took the easy way out here, and the script pays dearly for it.

Zhaan's checking out sequence is completely out of

character given what we know at this point. Her behavior will make perfect sense after we see "Dream a Little Dream," but here, she just seems psychotic. She has never been portrayed as weak or dependent, and yet when Moya is attacked, she's screaming for D'Argo to help them. In addition, the director completely missed an opportunity to align (if only momentarily) Zhaan and Aerny in the scene where Zhaan tells Aeryn she loves her. Unfortunately, the director decided to play that as an "Ewww!" moment instead of an emotional revelation and it comes off as homophobic at best. Even though by the scene's end it's clear what Zhaan is getting at, it is an ugly misstep.

Why have the powers that be decided Zhaan would be somehow more interesting if she used Americanisms like "you all" and flattened her accent almost to the point of invisibility? Zhaan's speech patterns were and are unique and it's baffling why the creative team decided to change this for the second season.

Zhaan's wardrobe also takes a pounding. While she's been seen in a golden corset worn on the outside of her clothing (which will be recycled in "Vitas Mortis," by the way) in past episodes, the costume designer has put her in what looks like a canvas tent. It's unflattering at best and ends up looking like a last minute, "Oh, here just wear this!" decision.

And speaking of wardrobe and makeup, there are a number of other noticeable changes to many of the characters. D'Argo's makeup has been radically altered. While this allows more of the actor's features to be seen (and thus more facial expressions are possible), it also makes his nose look unfortunately like a piece of latex. Although the kind of body-altering makeup that actor Anthony Simcoe had to wear in Season 1 was both uncomfortable and time-consuming to apply and take off, he looked wholly alien. The choice to cut down on D'Argo's facial makeup and cover up Zhaan so they don't have to take the time or expense to apply her body makeup make it seem as though the show's budget was severely slashed and one of the places they've cut corners is here.

Chiana's two-piece costume from Season 1 has also been altered into a one-piece affair with a body suit underneath the printed pants and top that closely matches her skin color. This choice was made, one would guess, so that makeup wouldn't have to deal with the expanse of skin at Chiana's midriff, but at certain angles, one can see the material twisting and if it's supposed to look like her skin, it doesn't.

She's also lost the cadence in her speech and the inflections have been flattened much like Zhaan's so that she is beginning to sound like the Americanization of Chiana. As with Zhaan, this is not necessarily a good thing. Losing the "accent" also means the actor has to re-find the vocal patterns that helped distinguish Chiana in the first place. And while Ms. Edgley does a fine job, as always, it's clear the dialogue coach wasn't much help here.

Aeryn's had a bit of a makeover as well, though costume-wise she will fare better as the season progresses, especially in terms of the leather ensemble which will become a trademark. But the hairstylist has given her a henna rinse which is not at all as attractive as the actor's own luscious dark color, and instead of brushing her hair back from her forehead, someone decided it would be better parted down the middle. If you're twelve, maybe.

Aeryn's hair has always been a problem. While it's nice to see such lovely tresses flying free (and she is known as the Raven Haired Goddess on the boards), it's not very realistic. The topknot choice is not terribly flattering, though functional. Aeryn has been a Peacekeeper her whole life, a Peacekeeper with long hair at that. I find it hard to believe that the Peacekeepers would allow a soldier to wear her hair loose. Thus I find it hard to believe that Aeryn would not continue to wear her hair as she always had — wrapped in wet leather at the base of the neck. What would be so terrible about Aeryn keeping some of her Peacekeeper "attire?" She can't really be expected to forget all she's been for her entire life in a matter of months, can she? And this is a perfect example.

Rygel has changed as well. He's a new puppet, it seems. Careful observation of his face from Season 1 will show just how much he's been altered. The new streamlined design probably makes it easier for him to be manipulated.

In terms of editing and sound, there are problems here, too. The sound is very muddy, and some of the dialogue is completely lost. D'Argo's voice sounds totally different, though I suspect the actor has not changed his vocalizations. Given what I know about film production, my guess would be that the number of microphones in use during any given scene has been drastically reduced. For us here at home, this means that the depth of the sound — the resonance of D'Argo's voice, for example — is going to be lost. It also means that dialogue which is naturally lost on the cavernous sound stage is not picked up by a second, or third, microphone. Nor has it been looped, which means that it's re-recorded by the actors after the scene is shot and added during the editing process. Again, it points to budget cutbacks.

The smooth flow of the editing is much more choppy here and one wonders if some of the new producers have had a hand in this as well. Although this will work itself out by the third episode, "Taking the Stone," — as will Chiana's accent — the beautiful fluidity, the nice dissolves and the overall flow of the show is completely different. If one looks at the scene in "Family Ties" in which Chiana brings the others to share a meal and the meal sequence itself and compare it with any scene from "Mind the Baby," the changes will be markedly clear.

One of the aspects of "Family Ties" which underscored the emotional experiences of the characters was the music. Again, listen to the music in that scene and listen to most of "Mind the Baby." Here, too, is a noticeable change. (As an aside, the music from the meal sequence will pop up again in "Taking the Stone" at the very end of the episode. Listen for it.)

For a fan who waited months and months for not only the season finale, but also this first episode, I was terribly disappointed. Some of my mates who watch the show with me talked about how they weren't going to watch anymore. A few new recruits didn't understand what all the fuss was about. And I, quite honestly, couldn't tell them.

Grade: D

Episode 10203: Vitas Mortis
Location: Uncharted World in the Uncharted Territories
Guest Cast:
Melissa Jaffa as Old Nilaam
Anna Lise Philips as Young Nilaam
Writer: by Grant McAloon
Director: Tony Tilse

SYNOPSIS:
When D'Argo encounters another Luxan, he's thrilled. When he discovers she's an Orican, a priestess in Luxan culture and wants him to help her attain the next plane of existence through the Ritual of Passing, he is honored beyond belief. While they prepare for the ritual and enact it, Crichton remains planetside with D'Argo, acting as a kind of witness to this ritual for his friend.

Aboard Moya, Chiana is washing clothes. D'Argo's clothes. When Aeryn brings in a few of her own items, Chiana refuses to do her laundry, which annoys Aeryn and sets up some of the dynamics which will be futher developed in "Taking the Stone."

During the Ritual of Passing, the Orican, whose

name is Nilaam, senses an incredible energy in D'Argo. She feels suddenly revitalized and chooses instead to perform another ritual: The Ritual of Renewal. When the Ritual of Renewal is over, D'Argo is stunned to realize that Nilaam is not dead, but has been transformed into a young and quite beautiful Luxan female. Nilaam is thrilled and to show her gratitude, she promises to help D'Argo return home and also helps him "revitalize" (remember Matala's comment in "Back and Back and Back to the Future?")

While Crichton waits for the revitalization to be finished, Zhaan and Aeryn respond to Chiana's calls for help from the "laundry room." It seems that she's become stuck in the wash water, which has frozen around her legs up to the knee. Crichton returns to help. Aeryn, after chopping at the ice for a while goes in search of grenades, obviously angry that not only has Chiana refused to do her laundry, but she's has mucked up the washer as well.

D'Argo and Nilaam come to Moya, ostensibly to help, but the closer Nilaam is to Moya, the more damage she causes. There are numerous problems all over the ship, including one which sucks Rygel into a breech that's infected the inner hull. And he becomes the poster boy for hull breech filling spackle.

Eventually, everyone comes to the same conclusion: The vast wealth of power Nilaam felt in her ritualistic joining with D'Argo didn't come from him; it came from Moya. She has to be willing to give up her new-found youth and complete the Ritual of Passing or Moya, and all those aboard, will die.

Reluctantly, Nilaam agrees, knowing that this is the outcome which was meant to happen in the first place. D'Argo and Nilaam return to the planet. Once the Ritual of Passing is complete, Moya is restored to health; Chiana is freed and Rygel is rescued from the wall.

CRITIQUE:

What works in this episode is Anthony Simcoe's performance. He's finally given a chance to exhibit some of his fine acting talent and he embraces this episode wholeheartedly. From his awe at encountering an Orican, to his obvious pain when he persuades her to do the right thing and restore Moya, Mr. Simcoe really nails each moment in this script. His chemistry with both guest actors who play Nilaam (young and old) is palpable and it's a delight to learn more about Luxan traditions and culture.

This episode also had a lot of problems, ranging from character development to scientific holes. Aside from the fact that director Tony Tilse seems to have spent the week before he directed this episode watching every film John Woo ever made and decided to make this episode an homage to slow-motion, the most glaring problem is with Chiana — not the actor — but the way the writer's have portrayed her. She claims she's washing D'Argo's clothes because she "likes him." But there hasn't been any indication that she likes him any more than she likes the rest of them. In fact, one could argue that she "likes" Crichton a lot more than D'Argo. She didn't jump into D'Argo's arms when she learned he was alive (see "Mind the Baby), nor has she really had any significant scenes with him that would indicate they have anything other than a casual, friendly relationship. For her to be washing his clothes and then refuse to wash Aeryn's smacks of unfriendly competition between females for the attention of males, which is as offensive as it is stupid.

It's more likely and would have been more believable if she'd just been washing her own stuff (although she only seems to wear one outfit, despite their numerous visits to "commerce planets") and refuse simply because she's not going to do anyone's stuff but her own. Even washing Rygel's garments would have been more believable.

Both Aeryn and Zhaan here are totally underused. In fact, in the first two episodes, Zhaan is barely a presence, which is a real waste of talent. All the characters are fascinating and one can only hope that the producers won't fall prey to only giving screen time to the most popular character of the moment according to internet boards and fan mail. This is one of the problems Star Trek: Deep Space Nine ran into during its tenure — almost completely ignoring some members of the ensemble while granting more and more screen time to others. This is a very talented ensemble cast who work well together and it would be a real shame to sacrifice this in order to play the ratings game. If the writers and producers really want to insure their show's a hit, they should start paying more attention to the writing and editing.

There are also some real scientific holes here. The most obvious one is that Aeryn claims she can see Rygel's backside during her spacewalk to check out the hull but when the hull breech occurs and the camera follows a tool being sucked out into space, there's a tunnel between the inner wall (where Rygel is stuck) and the outer hull. Aeryn could not have seen his backside unless she'd crawled up the tunnel. And if his backside had been in space, it would have been subject to that whole vacuum problem. Since we rely don't know whether Hynerian physiology is able to survive in the vacuum of space for extended periods of time, as Luxans can, it's impossible to know how Rygel's backside really fared. But certainly exposure to that kind of intense cold for an extended period (remember Aeryn goes out on a space walk and takes a look at him, so we're not talking about a couple of minutes here) will result in tissue damage. If there was any kind of sun-like star giving off intense ultra-violet radiation, he also might have been blessed with quite a serious sunburn — but again it's hard to know since the information available to most of us relates to humans, not Hynerians. Additionally, how is Aeryn able to break off a piece of hull to bring inside?

After several hours of exposure to a frozen substance, it's doubtful that Chiana would not have exhibited some kind of frostbite, despite her alien physiology, and there's no indication she was even treated for exposure. And what about Nilaam's maps? She says she's going to help D'Argo get home and at that point in the story, she's so grateful to be young again, that it seems unlikely she'd be lying. Ultimately, while D'Argo's part of this episode was wonderful and well done, the connecting storylines don't fare as well at all.

Grade: C

Episode 10204: Taking the Stone
Location: A Burial Planet in the Uncharted Territories
Guest Cast:
Anthony Hayes as Molnon
Peter Scarf as Das
Michela Noonan as Vyna
Natasha Beaumont as Janixx
Writer: Justin Monjo
Director: Rowan Woods

SYNOPSIS:

While Crichton is busy trying to figure out how Moya's navigation system "works," he manages to short out some of her systems, annoying Pilot and leaving him essentially sensor blind. Just about the time Crichton gets his first electrical shock of the day, Chiana stumbles into the room telling him she needs to talk. He tells her she's too busy. She retreats to one of the workrooms and removes from her abdomen a pulsing disc stops pulsing, indicating to Chiana that her brother has died.

Grief stricken, she steals Aeryn's prowler and ends up on a graveyard planet. Crichton, Aeryn and Rygel go after her. While Rygel amuses himself with grave robbing,

Crichton and Aeryn follow the trail of Chiana's discarded clothing to a maze of underground tunnels which eventually bring them into contact with a much-transformed Chiana and the Clansmen.

Back on Moya, Rygel's theft is uncovered, much to the consternation of D'Argo and Zhaan. She chants to protect him from revenge by evil spirits, but he throws her out and continues to revel in his greed.

Chiana, who has fully embraced their rituals which include running naked through rings of fire, eating "poisoned" mushrooms (ala Alice in Wonderland), drinking liquor from a jug as if she'd been running a backwoods still her entire life and calling everyone one Moya "lame." She wants Aeryn to stay and party with her, but Aeryn refuses. She flips the life disc back at Chiana and is gifted with the story of Chiana's brother and the news of his death. She asks Aeryn to at least stay for The Gathering and probably feeling a bit remorseful, Aeryn agrees.

In the meantime, Crichton has run into Molnon, an influential member of one of the Clans who live in this underground world. He arrives with Molnon and Das at the edge of a cliff and finds Aeryn and Chiana and several other Clansmen have gathered there, too.

The Gathering then commences and one by one, four Clansmen hurl themselves from the cliff edge and are miraculously saved from death by what Aeryn recognizes as a sonic net, an energy field created from one's own vocal patterns. Das' turn to jump arrives. Apparently, he doesn't have the right resonance the field requires and dies upon impact. Crichton and Aeryn are horrified; Chiana is fascinated and the stoned Clansmen regard it as all part of the normal routine.

Meanwhile, back on Moya, Rygel's plunder has begun to exhibit signs of enchantment and he is finally convinced, after being pinned to the wall by what look like giant gem-encrusted push pins, to restore his plunder to the grave from whence it came.

Chiana is bent on "taking the stone" — the leap into the chasm. Crichton tries to talk her out of it, uncovering, in the process, the reason for the Clansmen's short lives. It seems that they're being exposed to high levels of radiation which is augmented by the rocks in the chasm. The radiation sickens them relatively quickly, resulting in a painful and extended death. He tried to talk them into moving to the surface, but they refuse. And so does Chiana. In the end, she takes the stone, survives and is able to move forward in her grieving process.

Chiana buries the life disc on the planet's surface while Rygel returns the stolen grave goods and all return to Moya, one happy family once again.

CRITIQUE:

Writer Justin Monjo seems to have drawn from many different sources here in creating this episode. First, as many scifi fans probably noticed, the Clansmen's world was strikingly similar to the one found in Mad Max Beyond Thunderdome. Specifically, the cadences in the speech (a tendency to reverse subject and predicate), the youth-oriented culture, the cultish fascination with death stick out as the most obvious of these "borrowings." The idea of death at the onset of "adulthood" is an idea that was also done quite well in Star Trek (the original series a.k.a. TOS) in an episode called "Miri." (As a side note, Chiana's brother's name is a close sound-alike.) There, the children became horribly disfigured and then hopelessly insane at the onset of puberty. Here, Monjo has extended the timeline a bit further and made the cut-off point twenty-something when young adults begin to realize there may be more to life than snowboarding and drinking beer, or in this case when the realize there may be something more than "taking the stone."

Monjo's understanding of peer pressure and the desire to conform that so shapes a typical adolescent's experience is quite well done: Chiana reminding Crichton that he told her she was free to leave at any time, her desire to stay with these people who are closer in age to anyone on Moya save perhaps D'Argo, her anger at Crichton when he comes to retrieve her, her calling everyone on Moya "lame," insinuating that they're all essentially "old fogies," embracing a sub-culture (in this case, literally) dedicated to drugs, drinking and death-defying acts are all classic earmarks of adolescent rebellion. Additionally, Crichton's surprise and indignation when told the council will not embrace his logical, adult idea about moving to the surface in order to prolong their lives is much like a shocked parent's response to an adolescent child's choices which he or she doesn't necessarily agree with.

While on the one hand I liked with the writing team's choice to place Chiana as a younger member of the crew, I am not terribly thrilled with how they've set up John and Aeryn as her "parents." This grates against Chiana's overt sexuality and makes lines like her insinuation that she'd be John's bedmate only in his "dreams" seem like mixed messages. And even though there's more overt physical contact between John and Aeryn in the end of "Mind the Baby," they have still not been presented as a couple. Chiana, who is very clearly presented as the rebel, sexually adventuresome, sexually active female is being set up more and more as the "whore" to Aeryn's "Madonna." Chiana will be openly called a slut (among other terms of "endearment" later this season). Although it is clear that Aeryn struggles to overcome her PK upbringing and the way it has discouraged her from forming close emotional ties with anyone, on the very base level the creative team is setting up Aeryn as the more "pure" and "virginal" of the two women, even though I personally doubt Aeryn is either. And thank God for that! If we're going to be true to human nature, let's at least be honest about it. Perhaps the creative team's thinking is that Chiana is the girl you f—, but Aeryn is the one you marry.

It's also dangerous to portray her as a child because clearly she's managed to take care of herself and, if we weren't sure before, we are left with no doubts after this episode that she is sexually active. I have never been bothered by Chiana's sexual interplay with John. Given her personality and background, this is one of the ways she's learned to survive. And as we see so poignantly in "Family Ties," it is a way she knows how to give back. Rather than seeing her as a sexual object, Crichton is wisely allowed to see her as a well-meaning, but somewhat confused young woman who has the tendency to get them into trouble. And he treats her accordingly — sometimes with gentleness, sometimes with frustration. But drawing the lines so clearly here between "parent" and "child" relegates Crichton and Aeryn into dangerous territory — one that may not allow them to fully explore their own relationship without being seen as parental figures.

Aeryn, again wearing mostly leather with just enough midriff showing to give Chiana a run for her money, is largely wasted here. Her annoyance at being seen as ancient by the Clansmen seemed like a mysogonistic jibe at women's concern about their looks. Her tight-ass reaction to the offer of sharing a drink with Chiana, her comments that Chiana seems drunk enough already and insuation of irresponsibility all portray her as a disproving parental figure. And given what's been set up so far, it makes little sense. Regardless of whatever the actors' real ages are, Aeryn and Crichton, like D'Argo, are portrayed thus far as twenty- or, at most, thirty-somethings. The fact that Aeryn let Molnon's remark affect her at all was an other nail in the parental coffin, so to speak. She and John have to be seen now as "older" if they're going to be taken seriously as authority figures.

Rygel, Pilot, Zhaan and D'Argo don't have much to do in this episode and the "B" story isn't very engaging.

Although the scene between Zhaan and Rygel in which she tries to prevent him (and perhaps the others as well) from falling prey to a nasty post-mortem curse allows Ms. Hey a few fine moments, this subplot really only reinforces Rygel's greed — as if we weren't clear on this point already — and allows the props department to make a pretty good replica of the Sutton Hoo mask. This mask, which Rygel stole from one of the graves, neatly connects with the Clansmen's limed hair which was one of the characteristics of the early Celtic warriors. That the Clansmen see themselves as something of a warrior clan in not particularly clear, but the body painting and the hairstyle are definitely reminiscent of those ancient peoples. All that was missing was a golden torque.

Ultimately, what works in this episode is Ms. Edgley's performance. In the first two episodes of Season 2, the creative team seems uncertain about the character and neither the speech patterns nor mannerisms match the smooth alien-ness of Season 1's Chiana. "Taking the Stone" is the first episode of the season that harkens back to the old Chiana — the one whose intriguing fluid movements are so well embodied by Ms. Edgley and whose vocal patterns, accent and delivery set her apart from the other characters.

One has to wonder though about the life disk. If it's been in her body for so long receiving a signal from her brother — wherever his is — hasn't it also been emitting one as well so that he would know about her? You'd think that Scorpious would have made use of that. And when exactly does the brother die? When the disk's light goes out? When she stumbles into command? And if dies before she removes it, why does the light go out after?

Crichton is a stranger in a strange land. He should sound, look and behave differently from the other characters he encounters. It's a mistake to try and homogenize everyone by blending vocal accents to sound what essentially boils down to more "American." And hopefully, it's a mistake the creative team won't pursue.

But I'll leave you with a question: Why did John decide the best way to learn about Pilot's navigation system is by ripping it apart? Why doesn't he just ask Pilot how it works?

Grade: B-

Episode 10205: Crackers Don't Matter
Location: Aboard Moya in the Uncharted Territories
Guest Cast:
Wayne Pygram as Scorpius
Danny Adcock as T'raltixx
Written by Justin Monjo
Directed by Ian Watson

SYNOPSIS:

When a strange bug-like creature named T'raltixx comes aboard Moya with technology that promises to make Moya all but invisible to Scorpius, he's readily embraced by everyone except Crichton. For some reason, Crichton likens him to a used car salesman and is belligerent from the beginning. While T'raltixx's technology makes Crichton's module disappear quite effectively, he tells the crew the unit he has with him isn't large enough to hide Moya and that they must return to his homeworld so that he can procure a larger one.

This journey takes them through a series of five pulsars. T'raltixx warns everyone that the light may have an adverse effect on them and, aside from Zhaan, this proves true. Zhaan fares quite well throughout the journey as the pulsars' light engenders a continuous series of photogasms, the likes of which we have not seen since Season 1's "Till the Blood Runs Clear."

The rest of the crew, however, become distrustful of one another. Strange alliances form: Chiana and D'Argo,

Aeryn and Rygel. Squabbles erupt over crackers. Antagonism and mistrust among the crew escalates resulting in Aeryn barricading herself in the command center with Rygel, Pilot shunting in extra power and light to T'raltixx's quarters, D'Argo and Chiana attempting to steal Crichton's module, a near rape, an almost suicide and some of the most offensive and vile name-calling on the show to date.

Crichton manages to overpower all of his comrades and secure them in one of the hanger decks and then convinces them their real enemy is T'raltixx. Banding together like former enemies uniting to fight a common foe, each crew member (except Pilot) offers Crichton something to fight T'raltixx, from a hat soaked in regurgitated matter (from Zhaan) to a section from Aeryn's prowler to use as a shield. Crichton, looking like a bad imitation of a Superhero, goes after T'raltixx and kills him.

Once he's dead, the crew engage in overlong apologies, leaving the viewers wondering what the heck they've been watching for the last hour and thinking that wearing Zhaan's vomit would have been a more pleasant experience.

CRITIQUE:

To be honest, I can't remember the last time I encountered such a misogynistic and offensive episode of science fiction on television. And as far as the second season of the show goes, I'm starting to feel like a broken record. Although there were some wonderfully funny moments in this episode, most of it was complete garbage that should have been left in the writer's recycle bin.

There was no problem with the premise of the episode — a mysterious and somewhat untrustworthy alien with the promise of technology that proves too good to be true. His arrival splinters an otherwise unified crew and thus distracts them from his real purpose: The "friendly" takeover of their ship. If Justin Monjo had opted to stay away from misogynistic comments and repeated referrals to the shape and color of various characters' butts, he might have actually written a decent script.

Additionally, humorous moments helped the rising tension by giving us a chance to take a breath in between wondering whether everyone would survive. From Pilot's references to Zhaan's unabashed pleasure at being exposed to such intense light, to Zhaan's demanding that Moya not move an inch from her present position, to Scorpius' appearance in a gaudy Hawaiian-style shirt, to Pilot's critique of the human race and Aeryn's threat to turn Crichton into a salad topping, there were a lot of great one liners and clever exchanges.

There are also some really terrific moments of unspoken anger and tension. Probably the best is the silent conversation between Aeryn and D'Argo after D'Argo strikes Crichton. It's clear that D'Argo will strike another man without hesitation, but he won't hit Aeryn, despite the fact that she's a former Peacekeeper and a soldier. Aeryn coming to John's "rescue" is an interesting way to play the masculine/feminine in the Aeryn/John romance, too. The camera work as well as some of the makeup, most noticeably in terms of D'Argo, has also regained the flavor of Season 1.

But ...

I suppose the simplest way to dissect this episode would be to start with the opening sequence in which Crichton makes fun of T'raltixx's blindness in an obviously cruel way. Certainly this isn't necessary and if Mr. Monjo was trying to set up the conflicts that come later, he might have done it in a way that wasn't a classic example of human stupidity and childishness. All the women are referred to as either "bitch," or "slut" — except for Zhaan who just has a large blue backside (his words were more crass).   Crichton uses both of these "endearments" for Aeryn, in addition to calling her frigid. Are we to understand, then, that they've become lovers or was Aeryn just "frigid" in the one time they've been intimate in Season 1? And were they? Or was it all in Crichton's head? If they have become lovers, then this is certainly an inappropriate and ugly commentary on their physical relationship. And what is even more amazing to me is that the Another Universe site's critique of this episode pulled out this exchange as remarkable, but not for its offensiveness. I am personally stunned by what the vast majority of viewers, reviewers and creative team members for this show find acceptable in terms of women-hating, violent and a frankly abhorrent excuse for a script.

Chiana probably fares the worst of all the characters here. First, she's allied with D'Argo — perhaps in a continuation of the Chiana-does-laundry/Chiana-as-servant scenario from "Vitas Mortis." Then Crichton, who has been set up as a kind of father-figure in the previous episode, "Taking the Stone," pins her up against the wall, verbally assaults her in what quite honestly amounts to a rape and then to top it all off, becomes aroused at the thought of having "a little fun" with her after the others are dead. To say that I was disgusted and horrified at this scene would not even begin to express my revulsion.

This is probably the worst aspect of the episode but the writer's error is compounded in the apology coda in which Chiana cuts Crichton off as he tries to apologize and asks him where he came up with all that "crap" anyway. First of all, she would have never used this human term, "dren" would be more in character. Second, and more importantly, this is a major cop-out on the writer's part as it excuses Crichton's behavior and sends the message that it's okay or even cool to belittle someone with sexually charged slander and that a woman will forgive a man's little "slip" because he clearly wasn't in his right mind. This sends a dangerous message to the younger viewers of this show of both genders. It makes it seem like it's okay for a man to treat a woman he cares about by discussing her "performance" in bed (Aeryn) or using sexually violent language to frighten a clearly younger and in some ways more vulnerable female (Chiana). While I understand that we all have our dark sides and that perhaps it was somehow important for us to see that Crichton does as well, does not excuse this episode. That he can shoot his friend D'Argo in the leg and then kick him there to get his attention, that he calls his lover every detestable name in the book, that he gets off on the idea of sexual torture of a character who's been set up as a daughter-figure ... what was Mr. Monjo thinking? Was everyone out on a coffee break when the script was approved?

At the episode's end, the reasons behind what had affected the crew are still not adequately explained. Pilot says that "somehow" they were effected. But in scifi writing, that's just not good enough. Rygel probably sums up my feelings about this episode best when he tells D'Argo that he both can and cannot forgive him. Personally, I thought "Jeremiah Crichton" was the depths of stupidity from this creative team, but clearly I was wrong. While we may choose to forgive the creative team for this blunder and keep watching the show in the hopes that they'll get back on the right track, we cannot forgive the way in which the creative team allows the characters attack each other, the women-hating messages so clearly portrayed on the screen, the way the characters just "forgive" each other as if they'd collided in the corridor instead of nearly killing each other and causing emotional and physical damage.

Mr. Monjo manages to hit on the insidious nature of the disruption and how it impacts the crew several times. The scene in which Aeryn is holding a weapon to her own head and in her confusion seems perfectly at ease with the idea of shooting herself, for example, and the scene between D'Argo, Chiana and Crichton where D'Argo and Chiana are trying to steal Farscape 1 stand out. In the first instance, it seems almost probable that Aeryn will unwittingly commit suicide. The second instance highlights a sense of how the crew is trying to outguess and outmaneuver each other without success. Both of these scenes showcase the episode's point but without the sexual violence and overt cruelty exhibited in the other scenes.

But overall, this episode is a dismal failure. Perhaps Mr Monjo should take a vacation from writing for a while, or at least a walk on the beach to re-examine his responsibilities as a writer for a show of this caliber, the powerful nature of television's overt and implied messages and his own humanity.

Grade: F

Episode 10206: Picture if You Will
Location: Commerce Ship in the Uncharted Territories
Guest Cast:
Chris Haywood as Maldis and Kyvan
Writer: Peter Neale
Director: Andrew Prowse

SYNOPSIS:

If the Ferengi knew about the Uncharted Territories, they'd fall over each other in an effort to get a piece of the action. Commerce planets are so abundant Moya's crew encounter a new one practically every other week. And now, come to find out, there are commerce ships as well. If only Quark were here ....

Aside from Ferengi greed and an uncanny ability for self-preservation (which seems to have manifested itself quite nicely in Rygel), the next "worst" thing in the Uncharted Territories is probably letting Chiana loose to shop. After the fiasco that began "Crackers Don't Matter" where all Chiana had time to buy were crackers, one would have thought she'd be banned from all future excursions.

So when Rygel and Chiana — the two crew

members most likely to get into trouble -- visit Kyvan's commerce ship, it is inevitable that something will go awry despite the fact of Aeryn's escort. Chiana comes upon a painting that actually changes to reflect her face as well as a necklace she lost aboard Moya some time ago. Completely taken with the painting, she's overjoyed when Kyvan gifts it to her. Upon returning to Moya, the necklace suddenly reappears. Chiana, convinced that the painting has some kind of magical ability, is fascinated as it alters again, this time showing Chiana with a broken leg. Moments later, she trips over a DRD . . . and breaks her leg.

By this time, Crichton is more than a little concerned about the painting's strange ability to predict or perhaps cause future events and, reluctantly, Chiana allows Zhaan to take a small sample for analysis. Before Zhaan can make any clear determinations, however, the picture shows Chiana engulfed in flames.

Terrified and immobile, Chiana screams for help, claiming she can already feel her body heating up. She's rushed to a freezer compartment where everyone thinks she'll be safe, but moments later the compartment fills with fire. Unable to break down the door, the crew watches helpless and horrified as their comrade is consumed.

They are finally able to open the hatch, but all that's left of Chiana is a small pile of ash. Frightened and grief stricken, the crew members retrieve the painting only to find an image of D'Argo impaled, they assume, by his own sword.

A short time later, D'Argo is pierced, not by his sword, but by the business end of the Prowler. He disappears. This time, however, there are no remains.

As the crew becomes more and more terrified, John is "killed" and we come to realize that the crew members are not dead, but imprisoned. Maldis, the evil sorcerer from "That Old Black Magic" has somehow managed to pull his tiny microscopic pieces back together and is out for vengeance.

While Rygel and Aeryn try and find Kyvan's commerce ship to get more information about the painting, Zhaan is left alone on Moya to work frantically at finding a way to retrieve her comrades. Eventually, she, too, becomes the focus of Maldis' ugly destructive energy. Sucked into his world of horrors, she is at first overwhelmed by his power. Crichton, however, finds Maldis an almost laughable enemy compared to the torture he endured at Scorpius' hands.

Zhaan does manage to put all the puzzle pieces together and pull the various members of the crew into alignment. Rygel and Aeryn destroy Kyvan and the Commerce ship. Zhaan opens a kind of portal between Maldis' prison and Moya, and Crichton, D'Argo and Chiana manage to slip through. Maldis, however, then makes use of the portal and shoves a gigantic King Kong-like hand through the opening. Zhaan, using a hand-held DRD and a few back-up weapons, blows up the portal and sends Maldis out into space once more.

CRITIQUE:

As a way to give Zhaan some story and screen time, this episode worked. The exploration of the ways she wrestles with the two halves of herself, the power she draws on to defeat Maldis, the obvious hatred she has for him and his manipulative ways is well realized, largely due to Ms. Hey's talents.

As a story, there were some nice moments. There were some fantastic special effects, especially in the "corridor" of archways. Chiana and D'Argo, though also imprisoned in this reality, appear in much altered form — upside down or hugly enlarged — and the black water and rocks surrounding the corridor was a wonderful effect.

The painting, however, was a real disappointment.

Although it was great to see it shaping the future, the literal depiction of the character's deaths was very flat and Chiana's broken leg was outright comic book art laughable. A more interesting choice would have been for the painting to be more surreal or symbolic — this would have also heightened the tension. But perhaps the creative team was afraid we wouldn't "get it." Additionally, having Zhaan close the portal with — essentially — one DRD looked incredibly stupid. Here's this amazingly powerful sorcerer who has managed to reassemble his molecules and she's able to defeat him with one tiny DRD and one blast from the Prowler's weapons. Well, no. It just didn't seem realistic.

Rygel and Aeryn don't have much to do here, either, though it is fun to see Aeryn kicking butt and having a few really nice body shots as well. Isn't leather delicious? As Chiana, Ms. Edgley is phenomenal here at portraying child-like curiosity about the painting and later fully-realized terror when she's convinced she's going to die. If anyone stands out performance-wise here, it's Ms. Edgley, even though the episode really should have been more focused on Ms. Hey and Zhaan. Her confrontations with Maldis were wonderful, despite some weak writing, especially the scene in which he literally walks up her back and over her head. Great use of a symbolic act to convey power.

Additionally, what ultimately happens to the painting? The last image we see of it contains Zhaan. Does it disperse when Maldis is defeated at the end? Why was Chiana's necklace left behind when she disappears but there is nothing left of either D'Argo or Crichton? Although one could argue it's for dramatic effect — nothing left but that which would not burn — it's inconsistent.

One has to wonder why the creative team needed to make Kyvan look like an example of a badly aging drag queen. If Maldis is so powerful, why not just make himself look like a woman or a young man with different features.

I don't think the Maldis/Kyvan connection would have been lost on any of the viewers and this choice was gauche.

Grade: C-

Episode 10207: The Way We Weren't (Forgive and Forget)

Location: Aboard Moya.
Three years prior and present day
Guest Cast:
Alex Dimitriades as Lieutenant Velorek
Lani Tupo as Captain Crais
Writer: Naren Shankar
Director: Tony Tilse

SYNOPSIS:

Chiana shows Crichton a tape made three years earlier aboard Moya. He's more than a little unnerved. The tape, which shows Aeryn participating in the murder of Moya's original pilot, spotlights what they struggle to forget: That Aeryn was a Peacekeeper and bred to follow orders, no matter how personally distasteful she might find them to be. Chiana and John decide it's best to show the tape to the rest of the crew, but agree that Pilot should not view it. Zhaan, D'Argo and Rygel all respond to this new bit of information with a renewed hatred for Peacekeepers and viciously strike out at Aeryn. Zhaan and Rygel, in particular, are outraged and wonder whether Aeryn had participated in any of their many torture sessions since they were all prisoners by that time. Aeryn counters by reminding them they cut off one of Pilot's arms not too long ago in a self-serving attempt to go home.

Crichton supports Aeryn and his support allows her to cautiously relate her side of the story. She tells him that she'd been transferred from Prowler Detail to Transport Detail and met Lieutenent Valorek, a fellow Peacekeeper who had a gift when it came to understanding the symbiotic relationship between leviathan and pilot. The original pilot, who had been bonded to Moya for over twenty cycles, had refused to participate in any Peacekeeper experiments. Captain Crais, impatient to advance a secret pet project, had ordered the original pilot removed. When Valorek didn't act swiftly enough to suit his purposes, Crais ordered the troops present in the chamber to kill her.

Aeryn was one of those troops. Her grief regarding the death of the original pilot opens the way for additional revelations and Aeryn tells John that she and Valorek were lovers. Central Command, she explains, understands the needs of its troops. But the unspoken rules stated that none of the relationships could be conducted openly and long term relationships were discouraged. Central Command, because it controls both procreation and assignments, would never tolerate rank and file soldiers engaging in any sort of relationship that might get in the way of them being used like mere pawns in a cosmic chess game.

But Velorak was different, she admits. He was open in both expressing his affection for her and his desire to form a more permanent liaison. He shares with her the knowledge that he can intercede on her behalf regarding her next assignment. He also is dangerously candid about his feelings for Crais' secret project, which he finds abhorrent.

Around this same time, Rygel decides to show Pilot the tape and Pilot demands to see Aeryn. He is livid with rage and tries to kill Aeryn by strangling her. When Crichton intervenes and saves Aeryn's life, Pilot decides he will not move Moya another metre as long as Aeryn is aboard. Aeryn decides to leave, but not before allowing Zhaan to treat her bruised neck. Zhaan verbally attacks Aeryn again for her past actions, claiming she lacks compassion. Crichton, obviously distressed that everyone is complacent about Aeryn's departure, goes to talk to Pilot. In a fit of rage, Pilot physically disconnects himself from Moya.

Meanwhile, the flashback sequence continues. As the team works to put the new pilot in place, it becomes horribly clear that Crais' desire to complete his project will have devastating effects on both leviathan and pilot. Because the natural bonding process between pilot and leviathan usually takes one to two cycles but is being condensed into little more than sixty arns, Pilot will experience a high degree of pain, a side effect of the telescoped bonding which is permanent. Additionally, once Moya awakens and realizes what has happened, she is terrified. It takes some time for Pilot to become even primitively acclimated and to also learn how to "dumb down" his thoughts -- which according to Velorak -- can transmit more than one hundred images, ideas and concepts at a time. By this point, Velorak has managed to sabotage Crais' project.

Aeryn overhears the plan and when she confronts Velorak with the knowledge, he refuses to back down. Moments later, Crais and several other Peacekeepers enter the quarters where they've been together and Velorak is arrested for treason. Aeryn, seeing an opportunity to return to Prowler Detail, has betrayed him. Crais tells her to see Lieutenant Teeg (who you will remember was killed by Crais in "That Old Black Magic") for reassignment and Valorek is taken away.

They never broke him, Aeryn tells Crichton and even as he was being taken, he commended her on her intellect and her willingness to take risks. She realizes now that Crais' secret project was to breed a gunship/leviathan hybred. Valorek placed the shield which prevented conception. The same shield D'Argo accidentally broke in "They've Got a Secret."

By this point, Crichton and Aeryn have reached Pilot's chambers and after Crichton and Aeryn disarm the

DRDs, Pilot confesses to Aeryn that it was his own self-loathing that made him angry enough to order her off the ship. Valorek, he says, came to his homeworld looking for a pilot for Moya, knowing that he would not be able to convince Moya's original pilot to participate in Crais' project. Although Pilot had been turned down for a leviathan bonding due to his youth and inexperience, his desire to experience space travel was so strong that he agreed to accompany Valorek.

By doing so, he believes he signed the first pilot's death warrant. His guilt comes from the knowledge that maybe, if he'd refused, Valorek never would have found a replacement pilot and Moya's original pilot would still be alive. Both Crichton and Aeryn assure him that is not true, that the original pilot's refusal to participate in Crais' project resulted in her death. Finally, they convince Pilot to let them begin the bonding process again so that it can evolve naturally and Pilot will not be in constant agonizing pain. Aeryn and Pilot, who share both DNA and a troubling past full of regret, loss and self-hate, begin the long process of forgiveness.

CRITIQUE:

On some satellite systems and cable listings, this episode was entitled "Forgive and Forget." That, frankly, is a better title considering that the truth of this episode is about the way events and people were, not the way they weren't. As an aside, this episode was also produced before "Picture if You Will" but aired after in the USA. The BBC aired the episodes in the reverse order.

This episode is pretty evenly balanced in terms of what works and what doesn't. What works principally is the decision to present a huge chunk of backstory for both Aeryn and Pilot. The dissolves between past and present (the use of the image of a tape "fuzzing out" in the opening teaser and negative images in the body) visually augment this choice, as does the stark almost black and white feel to the lighting in the flashback sequences and the "warmer" feeling the lighting has in most of the present time sequences.

As Crichton tells Aeryn in the premiere episode, he believes she can be more than just a PK drone. Valorek, interestingly, said the same thing. Perhaps Aeryn just had to hear it twice to believe it herself. And similarly, her feelings for Valorek were new and strange enough to her that her rejection of him comes as no surprise. It's hard for viewers to remember from week to week (myself included), that Aeryn is a perfect example of someone who is a textbook example of a product of her environment.

Peacekeeper High Command acknowledges and even encourages sexual liasions between troops. They have obviously found it helps morale, even though the couples are not encouraged, or some might argue, even allowed to stay together. So while Aeryn is familiar with the territory of sexual intimacy, she's not familiar with the emotions that may accompany that intimacy. Her inability to recognize that what she felt for Valorek was love makes perfect sense. She had never seen "love." She'd never seen two adults who choose to be together because of an emotional and a physical connection. We all base our behaviors and choices — at least initially — on what we know, what's familiar and what we've witnessed. It's no surprise that Aeryn is extremely reluctant to let John into her emotional universe — and it's clear that for him, sex and love are connected, at least where Aeryn is concerned.

Aeryn's background and relationship with Valorek are interesting for several other reasons. Although she tells Crichton that she is the child of a love-based relationship, she clearly doesn't know what that means as a behavior model. Having Aeryn be the product of proscribed procreation would probably have been a more interesting choice — perhaps the creative team just wanted her to have some kind of common ground in terms of parental relationships to share with Crichton.

Perhaps Valorek was taken during a PK raid and this might account for his inability to swallow whole anything that High Command spits out. Valorek's willingness to defy Crais gives us a peek into a whole world of renegade Peacekeepers, an intriguing idea. He's also astute enough to know how to use the system to his own advantage in order to take Aeryn with him. In essence, he not only focuses her insight into how Central Command functions politically, but also provides her with that special something she needs to stand out from her fellow grunt soldiers.

Aeryn's grief upon viewing the tape, her defensiveness with the others, her self-brutalization (both physically and emotionally) are all quite well realized in Ms. Black's performance. The scenes she shares with Crichton are particularly memorable. Crichton shows a bit more depth as well. One senses his jealousy regarding the intimacy Aeryn shared with Valorek (sexual and otherwise), but it also seems to give him hope that she might one day feel the same way toward him -- or if she already does love him, be able to express it. His gentleness in the scenes where she talks of her past are a nice change from the standoffishness and frustration with her he's been exhibiting of late. As a stepping stone in their relationship, it creates solid footing for further intimacy, especially emotional.

For the many fans of Pilot, this episode is an outright joy. So much information is presented here, it takes several viewings to take it all in. The CGI in these scenes is really amazing. Watching Pilot being lowered from the ceiling reminds us again how huge he is in comparison to the others and how different a creature. Note how he survives on his world in a mist-covered pool and then watch again the scene in which Valorek extracts the fibers which will create the symbiotic relationship. Pilot, as we'll see again in "Out of Their Minds" is not a biped, but dependent for mobility upon a leviathan, just as the symbiots in the Star Trek universe depend upon the race of Trills to provide them with a physical form in which to experience the world.

The vast and complex intelligence that we've sensed in Pilot all along is also given some screen time. Valorek's remark that a single sentence in his language can convey more than one hundred thoughts, emotions and concepts gives us just a small idea of how many tasks, ideas and more he's capable of at any given moment. This will be explored again in a different way in "Out of Their Minds" and it's nice to have the setup here to build on.

Since Talyn will figure prominently again in the four episode season finale and has been a huge part of the overall story arc, it's no surprise to find Captain Crais in the murky depths of this story. The hybrid breeding project seems to have more layers than initially revealed. Why Crais lied about prior knowledge of the project early in Season 2 is not clear, but his involvement in the project from its outset puts a completely new spin on his single-minded search for Moya. Perhaps his brother's death was merely his cover story —although he certainly seems to honestly grieve for him in "That Old Black Magic." Perhaps what he wanted all along was to retrieve the rogue leviathan and pursue the project on his own.

One of the questions raised but not fully answered concerns how leviathans breed. Aeryn says Crais wanted to impregnate the leviathan. Valorek's subterfuge was to place the conception shield (I guess it really should be called an anti-conception shield). D'Argo breaks the shield which results in Moya's pregnancy. So are we to conclude that she was already impregnated but the "sperm" (for lack of a better term given that Moya is referred to as female) was inactive? Or are leviathans hermaphrodites, possessing both male and female sex organs and the ability to procreate independently? I would guess the latter is true, but since Crais' project most certainly involved changing Moya's DNA enough to produce a hybrid never seen before, we cannot be absolutely certain at this point how the hybrid came to be.

This is not the only logic hole in the episode, either. Since Pilot can see and hear everything that goes on aboard Moya (as we have seen previously several times), it doesn't really work for the tape to be a secret. Chiana does not make any attempt to secure the room before showing Crichton the tape, nor do they do the same before sharing the information with the others. Additionally, if Pilot says that he was aware of everything going on around, why didn't he recognize Aeryn the moment she boarded Moya and removed her helmet in the first episode? Aeryn also claims to have been aboard many leviathans, but this situation seemed different enough that she would remember. Does that mean all leviathans look alike and all the ones she was stationed on also carried prisoners? Does it mean that the leviathan breeding program took place on many ships? It's clear this is Valorek's final assignment and they had not known each other previously. Her story, though believable on some level, feels more like defensive posturing than truth. But the creative team has dropped in clues like this before, so perhaps there is something more to this inconsistency than is readily apparent.

Although no one can deny the emotional, physical and psychic damage of torture, the crew members' reactions to the tape seems hypocritical. Chiana, for example, was a Nebari prisoner, not a Peacekeeper one. Rygel's outrage, given what had transpired between him and Aeryn in "Durka Returns" seemed extreme.

Zhaan takes delight in hurting Aeryn both physically and emotionally as she's treating Aeryn's neck but when Aeryn calls Zhaan on her remark, asking her bluntly if Zhaan thinks she has no compassion, Zhaan does a complete reversal, apologizing and reassuring Aeryn that she could not have been any different back then. Why wasn't this as obvious to Zhaan right off as it was to the rest of us? Zhaan must know that for Aeryn to leave is extremely dangerous, as dangerous as it would be for Zhaan to depart and attempt to evade the Peacekeeper Paddoc Beacons for the rest of her life.

At times, it seems as though the creative team can't decide how to play Zhaan. Although clearly a complex character with many levels of experiences, passions and dark impulses, she often comes off, especially in Season 2 as overly fragmented, as though the writers can't agree about her basic characteristics enough to present her as a consistent character. There's a difference between complexity and consistency — and this is an important example of how the two of those sometimes get transposed.

Initially, D'Argo is equally self-righteous, but later he tells John that he has no memory of this event — or any other for that matter — because he spent the term of his imprisonment chained to the wall of his cell, which explains (for the second time, actually) the presence of the rings in his collarbones. So why get hot and bothered?

These reactions don't work. As Aeryn reminds them, they were all only too happy to cut off one of Pilot's arms in "DNA Mad Scientist" for the promise of map crystals. Their outrage over Aeryn's actions, especially given that for her to have refused a direct order would be completely out of character for a Peacekeeper born into the ranks, not kidnapped, lacks any kind of empathy for how hard it has been for her to adjust. Everyone aboard Moya has lost something of great emotional value and ganging up on Aeryn and blaming her for something over which she essentially had no control comes off as a foolish device to further the plot. What was the motivation here? To push John and Aeryn closer together? To align them against the rest of the crew? To split the crew into factions?

One last note, pay particular attention to the top of your screen during the initial scenes between John and

Chiana. Is that the top of the set I see before me? ;)

Grade: B+

Episode 10208: Home on the Remains
Location: Rotting Budong Carcass
Guest Cast:
John Brumpton as B'Soog
Justing Saunders as Altana
Rob Carlton as Vija
Hunter Perske as Temmon
Gavin Robins as Keedva
Writers: Gabrielle Stanton and Harry Werksman, Jr
Director: Rowan Woods

SYNOPSIS:

Just when the food supply has dwindled to the point where Crichton is reduced to frying and attempting to eat dentics, Moya and her crew finally arrive at the Budong carcass Chiana has been going on about. She claims that there's a mining colony where they'll be able to get supplies. Aeryn argues for trying someplace else, but Zhaan makes it clear that if she doesn't eat soon, she will die.

Zhaan is beginning to metamorphose as a result of their near starvation, and this transformation is creating problems for the other crew members who are having violent allergic reactions to the plant spores Zhaan is sending into the air. Everyone, that is, except Aeryn. She complains that she's not very happy about being stuck with a blooming shrubbery while Crichton gets to go off and play with his "chippy" (a.k.a. Chianna). But her protests fall on deaf ears.

Planetside, Chiana tells the others that Temmon will help them procure food, but moments after they arrive Temmon is wheeled out of the mine, near death. He begs

Chiana to put him out of his misery. She does, much to Crichton, D'Argo and Rygel's collective surprise. But Temmon's brother, B'Soog, praises her audacity.

With Temmon gone, Chiana approaches B'Soog; he agrees to feed all but Chiana. B'Soog is still angry that Chiana chose Temmon over him and then stole from Temmon before fleeing. B'Soog gives the three males vegetables, but tells them that if they want to eat meat, they'll have to pay for it. And the only form of payment he accepts is in the form of crystals called nigeltee (this is a phoenetic approximation of the spelling of this word)* which are quite abundant in the rotting carcass.

B'Soog, however, has closed the mine until he can investigate his brother's death and deal with the Keedva, a violent creature who feeds on the Budong and has been known to attack and kill miners. Because the creature is so vicious, the miners are spooked enough to follow B'Soog's orders. They don't seem at all concerned about a work stoppage. But for Crichton and the others, it seems an insurmountable problem.

Rygel decides that the best way to get what they need is to play a strategy game with the local gambler, Vija. Though both cheat outrageously, Vija proves a better thief and Rygel ends up owing him a significant amount of crystal.

In the meantime, the ever-resourceful Chiana is quick to take action on two other promising schemes. The first involves an old friend, Altana, who has finally found a vein of nigeltee large enough to get her off the rotting carcass forever. Her affection for Chiana is obvious and she generously offers to split the claim. But first they have to find their way into the mine. The second scheme is just as risky, but in a different way. Knowing that B'Soog finds her attractive, Chiana plays on his desire for her. Her seduction is interrupted by a very jealous D'Argo who goes so far as to threaten to kill B'Soog if he doesn't provide them with the meat they need.

B'Soog mocks Chiana by asking if the Luxan makes all her decisions for her, and she lashes out at D'Argo, pointing out that not only will she do whatever it takes to save Zhaan, but she's also managed to live by her wits before she met him and she doesn't need him to protect her now. D'Argo tells her that a brotherly relationship is not what he's looking for, but goes no further. Finally, Chiana relents and tells him about Altana's claim, confessing that they're afraid B'Soog will jump the claim before they have a chance to mine it. D'Argo agrees to go into the mines with Altana.

Crichton returns to Moya with food for Aeryn and Zhaan. When he tries to get the nearly comatose Delvian to eat, she grabs his hand, inflicting great pain, and explains to him in one of her last moments of lucidity that she's past the point where anything but animal protein will stop the metamorphosis. Apparently, when Delvians begin to starve, they become immobilized. Because they are so incredibly vulnerable in that state, they become food for predators. In order to survive, their bodies produce buds. Within these buds, poisonous spores reside and are released into the air. When a predator is poisoned and immobilized, the Delvians consume them and are able to return to their normal state. But if she doesn't get animal protein within a few arns, it will be too late.

Crichton returns to the planet's surface, determined to get meat at whatever cost, leaving Aeryn to cope with the increasingly deadly atmosphere on Moya. In the hopes that a burst of strong light will help Zhaan photosynthesize light into energy, Aeryn rigs up two sets of lights and turns them on. This, unfortunately, was exactly the wrong approach as it accelerates the process of Zhaan's transformation. The poisonous spores begin to affect Moya's systems. Aeryn and Pilot decide that if they can get Zhaan into one of the transport pods they can depressurize the ship and blow the spores out into space. But when Aeryn goes to find Zhaan, she's disappeared. Left to choose between Moya's life or Zhaan's, Aeryn tells Pilot to depressurize the ship save for Command. As the breathable atmosphere on Moya diminishes, Aeryn asks the presumed-dead priestess for forgiveness.

Meanwhile, back on the carcass, Crichton overhears Chiana trying to renegotiate with B'Soog. He refuses to budge, sticking with his earlier proposition that he would accept Chiana's life in exchange for Zhaan's. One night is not enough for him. She must stay until he is finished with her.

Angered and frustrated, she storms off. A few minutes later, she tells Crichton that D'Argo has gone into the mine with Altana and has not returned. Annoyed, Crichton goes into the mines after him but finds Rygel instead, chipping away at a vein of crystal so that he can pay Vija. Admonishing Rygel and telling him to get the heck out, Crichton continues to search for D'Argo, but encounters the Keedva instead. In the hilarious scene that follows, Crichton tries to clamber aboard Rygel's floating throne to avoid becoming the Keedva's next meal, but Crichton's weight drags them ever downward. A fit of hissing and spitting between Rygel and Crichton ensues with a fair amount of slapping and punching thrown in for good measure. Luckily, they manage to avoid becoming lunch.

Deeper inside the Budong, D'Argo and Altana have nearly finished loading a mining cart with crystal. They talk of Chiana. D'Argo confides that although he's attracted to Chiana, he feels he cannot trust her. Altana assures him that Chiana has a good heart, even though her loyalties do shift according to what's required for survival. Suddenly, they're attacked by the Keedva. Altana is mortally wounded. When she's brought out of the mine by D'Argo, he is close to tears when he tells Chiana that he did all he could to save her friend.

Moya is feeling much restored and repressurization is almost complete. Zhaan drops down from the ceiling in

Command and accuses Aeryn of deliberately trying to kill her. Aeryn is able to make one final appeal to the intelligence now almost completely buried beneath Zhaan's primitive survival instinct. For one moment, Zhaan's reason returns. Aeryn takes that opportunity to knock her cold with a PK head-butt.

B'Soog enters the mine to retrieve another slab of meat. Crichton follows him, discovering his hidden stash. He also realizes that B'Soog has managed to train the Keedva and is more than willing to use the animal to kill anyone who gets in his way. It seems clear now that his motivations are purely self-centered, so much so that he would sacrifice his own brother for the sake of gaining more crystal. He leaves Crichton to fend for himself against the Keedva when he hears Chiana's voice calling Crichton. Crichton manages to kill the creature.

Chiana, in the meantime, is holding B'Soog at gunpoint. Again he taunts her, calling her a thief and a slut, but not a killer. She hesitates, seems to back down, but fires the weapon suddenly, bursting open an acid-filled pustule directly behind B'Soog. In a truly disgusting horror movie fashion, we are treated to watching B'Soog's hand and arm dissolve and drop in bloody pieces to the ground. She leaves him in the tunnels screaming his lungs out.

Reunited aboard Moya, the crew celebrate Zhaan's recovery and their renewed food stores with a belt-loosening meal. Zhaan apologizes to Aeryn for accusing her of attempted murder and acknowledges that Aeryn was only trying to help. Chiana, stealing a moment for private mourning, is joined by D'Argo. He tells her that it's okay to relax, that she is among friends. She counters by saying that she can't relax unless she feels safe. He tells her she is. And then he kisses her.

CRITIQUE:

"Home on the Remains" is a good example of an

episode where both the A (main) and B (secondary) stories are nearly of equal weight and interest, and the writers (who are often credited as script supervisors for other episodes) do a good job here of creating a real ensemble feel to the story and keeping it tightly focused and cohesive.

Using Crichton as the link, literally and figuratively, between the two storylines does a couple of things. First, he is portrayed as the leader/father figure beginning in the opening teaser when he argues with Aeryn about whether they'll stay or go, continuing through the sequence in which he tries to feed Zhaan and including such defining moments as his complaining about how nothing is every easy and attempting to retrieve D'Argo from the mine. When D'Argo uses a give-me-what-I-want-or-I'll-kill-you approach, B'Soog meets him with stony opposition. Crichton, coming from a culture where he's more likely to get what he wants through brains rather than brawn, watches and waits until the time is right to make his move. His actions, ultimately, prove the most successful.

This distance is also useful in setting up the continuing development of the D'Argo/Chiana relationship. Crichton has to be clearly seen as not the love interest, although this has been made pretty clear in previous episodes, before D'Argo can approach Chiana.

Watching D'Argo fumble for words when Chiana asks him what he wants is a nice moment as well. Allowing him to be vulnerable reminds us he is a man who has already loved -- and lost. That Chiana doesn't recognize his jealousy and posturing for what it is tells us something about her as well, that she is slow to trust but quick to size up a situation and use it to her own advantage — an ability that has allowed her to recognize the danger in a culture that crushes individuality, flee from it and even manage to outwit her Nebari captor. She is determined to survive.

This desire comes into conflict with the other crew members' moral codes. At the end of "Durka Returns,"

Crichton tells her that if she's going to stay aboard Moya she has to follow certain rules. D'Argo confides in Altana that, although he is attracted to Chiana and willing to wait for her, he's troubled by her propensity for theft, lying, cheating and shifting loyalties. These are all valid concerns. As we've seen several times since Chiana has joined the crew, she's often more of a detriment than an asset. Producer David Kemper reminded fans in an August 2000 chat that although Rygel is annoying, he's also extremely smart. Chiana is also smart — not science-smart like Crichton, but survival smart.

I don't know if the other crew members' attitudes toward Chiana's mode of operation and the choices she makes are the result of the American tendency to take the high moral ground, especially where it concerns a woman using her sexuality to survive, but I am getting pretty tired of hearing Chiana called various versions of "slut." While B'Soog's comments seem aimed at getting Chiana riled enough to doubt her ability to kill him, Aeryn's complaint in the opening sequence is petty and just another attempt at fragmenting the women characters. John's not interested in Chiana — what difference does it make to Aeryn who travels to the carcass to get supplies? It seems that even in the Uncharted Territories if you're a woman, you're either a virgin or a whore. And guess who gets to fill the latter role here?

What burns me about this constant name-calling is the fact that neither Zhaan nor Aeryn are particularly virginal -- and shouldn't be. Zhaan, let us remember, killed her lover. Aeryn is quite honest about the fact that Peacekeeper policy allows troops to take as many lovers as they want whenever they want. What's the difference? A fine line.

Moralistic purists who view a woman's sexuality as both titillating and off-putting at the same time will argue that neither Zhaan nor Aeryn have "used" sexuality to survive. They will argue that Chiana "prostituted" herself.

But is Zhaan's crime any different in this context? She was using sex with her lover as a way to make him vulnerable so she could kill him. How is that different from Chiana trying to seduce B'Soog in order to procure food for her crewmates? And ultimately my feeling is, so what? Quite honestly, who cares?

Must we drag that tired old double-standard into the Uncharted Territories? Must we impose human moralistic codes on cultures that the creative team has gone to such pains to set apart? Pay attention to Crichton's behavior in the up-coming three-part story arc "Look at the Princess" and observe how seriously he takes his wedding vows. Why does no one call him a "slut" when he sleeps with another woman within twenty-four arns of his marriage. Perhaps monogamy doesn't apply in that case. Or perhaps it's just easier for the creative team to let themselves be lulled by the old offensive stereotypes rather than embrace the challenge. They've already crossed the PG-13 line in terms of sexual content and sexually suggestive situations (something that will become even more apparent in the next few episodes). Exploring different perspectives about adult sexual relationships would be fertile ground here. There's no excuse for this kind of laziness in the face of so much other ground breaking thinking.

Most Farscape viewers are familiar with the way in which many Western cultures make a lot of noise about monogamy, the sanctity of lovemaking, etc. But in other cultures, some African aboriginal tribes, for example, the practice of having many wives is as normal and expected to them as having a single wife is to Westerners. And they were just as confused by monogamy and in some ways appalled when Western culture ideas were first introduced — how does one secure the success and continuation of the tribe, especially the leader's familial line with only one wife? What if she can't have children? What if all her children die? Sexuality and marriage practices are all about context.

Unfortunately the creative team has decided that Zhaan's murder of her lover was justified because it was for a "greater good." Aeryn betrays her lover Valorek to Captain Crais because she wants to return to Prowler duty. But neither Aeryn nor Zhaan get called slut or whore. But Chiana is somehow relegated to the status of fallen woman. How does that follow? And does this mean that we're going to be treated to the whole Madonna/Whore dichotomy -- and I'm not talking about the pop star here, either. Zhaan has been largely portrayed as a non-sexual being. That leaves Aeryn as Madonna (maternal figure, big sister) and Chiana as ... well, you see where I'm going with this and I've gone here before. And to top it all off, Altana actually uses the oldest cliche in the book when she describes Chiana as having a heart of gold. The prostitute with a heart of gold. Now, where have I heard that before? I expected more from this team — they have written three strong, adult female characters. Why are they falling into this predictable and, frankly, offensive trap?

On another note, B'Soog's comment about having to use crystal to "pay" for meat gave us a little bit of insight into how goods are acquired. He claims the Budong is not a Commerce Planet when Crichton offers to trade medical supplies for food, but isn't using crystal to buy meat also a form of trade?

Director Rowan Woods seemed to have a problem deciding how he wanted to play the accents. B'Soog's accent is uneven, as is Vija's. And even though the official scifi channel site lists B'Soog's name as spelled with a double "o," everyone pronounces it as though it's "B'Saag." Were B'Soog and Vija trying to sound so American cajun?

Aside from the Chiana-as-slut problem, which is not going to go away, the episode has some really fine points. In terms of Zhaan's character developement, how wonderful it is to get to know more about her. We haven't received this much information all in one episode since

"Bone to Be Wild." And even though the result of Aeryn's attempts to help Zhaan don't work, the fact that she's honestly concerned about Zhaan's well-being runs in tandem with Chiana's maneuverings planetside.

There are also a few other bits that make this episode work. The Budong set was really wonderful. The feeling of the camp, the smoke, steam and grimy workers was the obvious product of the set designers' and crew members' attention to detail. My only complaint was that the floor of the inside of the carcass was too smooth. It looked like the floor of a set made out of cement, not a rotting carcass floating in space.

Additionally, casting Justine Saunders as Altana was brilliant. She was the perfect mix of friend, prospector and dreamer. Hers was a standout performance. And even though Crichton's calling Rygel "Maverick" is partially true — Maverick is a character from American film and television who was played by James Garner and fellow Aussie Mel Gibson respectively — Maverick was a charming and witty card shark who usually won. Rygel is certainly not charming, often not witty and in this case lost the game as well.

Overall this was a mixed episode with good character development in some areas but too much reliance on cliche in others.

Grade: C+

Episode 10201: Dream A Little Dream
Location: Planet Litagaria
Guest Cast:
Steve Jacobs as Ja Rhumann
Sandy Gore as Judge
Simone Kessell as Finzzi
Marin Mimica as Dersch
Peter Kowitz as Tarr
Jeremy Callaghan as Bartender

Writer: Steven Rae
Director: Ian Watson

SYNOPSIS:

Although this show aired in the eighth position in Season 2, it's actually numbered as 10201 and falls chronologically before "Mind the Baby."

While the fate of Crichton, D'Argo and Aeryn is unknown, Moya becomes anxious to search elsewhere for Talyn. But Zhaan, in particular, is determined to find her missing crewmates. While Rygel and Chiana generally make trouble and offer little help or support, Zhaan is aggressive in her search. So much so that she catches the eye of a slimy litagator named Finzzi who sees in Zhaan a perfect foil for a plan.

A short while later, Zhaan is arrested for a traffic violation and imprisoned. Distraught over not only the time she'll be expected to stay on Litagaria, but also the fact that she is once again behind bars, Zhaan experiences a series of visions of Crichton, Aeryn and D'Argo which call her sense of responsibility as well as her inner strength into question.

Enraged by the obviously biased system, Zhaan attacks her public defender. Later that night, Zhaan is freed by Finzzi. Zhaan doesn't stop to question her good luck. She simply flees. And when she's in sight of Chiana and Rygel, she trips over an object in the street and moments later is surrounded by police officers. Looking down, she sees that the object she tripped over is a body. Horrified, she realizes she's being charged with the murder of Wesley Ken.

In court the next day, Chiana and Rygel take over for the public defender who knows he can't possibly win Zhaan's case and doesn't want to share her fate, in this case a death sentence -- the outcome for lawyers who lose. Chiana and Rygel are completely inept. Zhaan withdraws and it seems that there's no way out.

But a kindly barkeep intervenes, providing Rygel with the Axiom, the small kernel from which this overgrown legal system has grown. With his help, Rygel begins to put together the truth of the case. Meanwhile, Chiana gets friendly with one of the police officers in order to extract information from him, which she uses without a single qualm later in the trial.

Threatened by Finzzi and her employer Ja Rhumann (who owns the "ruling" law firm of the moment), Chiana returns to Rygel feeling hopeless. He encourages her to play to their strengths — mainly deception and intrugue. And that's exactly what they do.

Using their own Axiom against them, Chiana and Rygel manage to implicate Ja Rhumann in the death of Wesley Ken, who was an advocate for the Utilities — Litagaria's serving class. Freed of suspicion, Zhaan and the others are allowed to leave.

CRITIQUE:

Although the "explanation" about the chronology versus the airing of this episode claims that the time directly following the Gammack Base's destruction was extremely chaotic, I suspect another, more insidious explanation.

After "Family Ties," I'm sure there were season wrap meetings, discussions of character popularity, etc. And I'm sure I'm not the only one who noticed the obvious use of the frame in this episode (Zhaan and John adrift in the transport pod) which allowed it to be shown completely out of sequence. Why were Zhaan and John on the pod together in the first place? It just comes off as an easy solution to get them together without any motivation. Additionally, since we know that Zhaan survives her ordeal on Litagaria and is reunited with the rest of the crew, one could argue that there's nothing at stake here. Whether she lives or dies is never a question throughout the entire episode. At best, we get to wonder whether they make a daring escape attempt or simply use the justice system to their own end.

What a sad commentary this is to the creative team's trust in their audience and in the power of this script! Did they think no one would watch if there was — gasp! -- one episode without John Crichton? Were they afraid that ratings would plummet as they had on The X-Files when Ms. Anderson went on maternity leave and one entire show aired with Mulder sans Scully?

Because of this decision, the impact of this episode in the larger story arc is completely wasted. Zhaan's fears about the fate of her crewmates, her willingness to sacrifice herself, her self-doubts and recriminations ... does this not make good story? Of course it does! And I wish the creative team would remember that we're intelligent out here and some of us can actually enjoy a show focusing Zhaan as much as we can one that focuses on any of the others.

Putting this aside however, let's look at the episode inside the frame.

Litagara. I shudder to think of living there. It's an interesting commentary on a legal system (be it American or other) that's grown too cumbersome to work properly. The idea of justice has been sacrificed on the alter of deception and creative presentation of the facts is something none of us want to think about very hard. Aside from the dinner plate the judge mistook for a hat, the costumes in this episode were extraordinary. Zhaan's prison garb, in particular, was so close to the uniforms worn by prisoners in WWII it was eerie. Additionally, the lighting really augmented the atmosphere — from the direct and unforgiving light in the courtroom to the muted claustrophobia of the cellblock. Catching Zhaan in the spotlight after her escape attempt, seeing her pinned in that terrible light was a startling and truly disturbing image. Light in this episode is both a physical element and a thematic one as the "Light of Truth" is what should be at the heart of every courtroom hearing.

It's clear that this trial is not about the truth. And this idea provides a framework for Zhaan's deep-seated fears about how others see her (as opposed to her inner truth). In her first vision, Zhaan admits that she draws her strength from the others (which now clarifies her emotional state in the opening sequence of "Mind the Baby"). She admits that she needs their help. That she needs to be "rescued" — both from this situation and from the darkness that has been unleashed inside her. Zhaan's withdrawal and strange behavior in "Mind the Baby" now make perfect sense.

Zhaan's second vision forces her to confront her doubts about leaving Aeryn, D'Argo and John. And in the third vision, she accepts a kiss from D'Argo and admits that she's not sure she has the strength to begin her spiritual quest again. The long struggle with controlling her darker impulses, the extended imprisonment and the stress of being on the run for the past cycle has finally taken its toll. We see Zhaan broken down and broken open, looking for answers and guidance instead of providing them.

Zhaan was such an incredible character at the beginning of the series. In these initial episodes of Season 2, she seems shrill and harsh. Is the result of re-initiating one's spiritual quest becoming perpetual shrew? Even her femininity is lost as the more revealing costumes of Season 1 have been transformed into several of the most unattractive gunnysack dresses I've ever seen. Why is it okay for Aeryn to run around in tight-fitting leathers and a vest that looks like it was made from remnants, and Chiana in something that fits so close it could be a second skin, but Zhaan is not allowed to be seen as the lovely female she is? This really cheats the character.

Ms. Hey does an incredible job here of embodying Zhaan's emotional range, especially during the vision sequences. Rygel, too, gets to show his softer side, holding Zhaan's hand in the moments before their final appearance in the courtroom. The puppeteers really worked this episode, so much so that I nearly forgot Rygel wasn't a living, breathing Hynerian, especially in the bar scene when he makes his "blue eyes" connection. Additionally, Ms. Edgley gets a chance to do some wonderful over the top theatrics after she takes three instead of one of Rygel's hangover cure pills. The rapid-fire delivery of her lines and the momentum she displays leaping around in the courtroom are one of the show's highlights. But what was up with the crotch shot when she's on the defender's table? If the director was going for that Look-I'm-suddenly-awake-now feeling, why shoot from this angle? Was that just a titilation shot for the target demographic?

In Season 2 thus far, it feels like about a hundred different people are writing Pilot's lines and no one can decide on how he's supposed to be played. He claims to get great pleasure out of serving others — and he says Moya does as well — but doesn't decide to stay around and help out until Moya overhears the conversation between Chiana and Finnzi. Zhaan's life has been endangered from the start, why this change of heart now?

It also didn't follow that a planet so encumbered by litigation would actually allow outsiders who were not lawyers to argue in their courtroom. This seemed unrealistic — just a useful device to get Chiana and Rygel into the action.

Had this episode been aired as the first of Season 2 without the Zhaan and Crichton frame, it would have been enormously powerful. Here, stuck nearly mid-season, it seemed like an afterthought. With strong performances like this, it was a real disservice to the actors, particularly to Ms. Hey, to relegate this episode as the eighth to air.

Grade: B-

Episode 10209: Out of their Minds
Location: Aboard Moya
Guest Cast:
Lani Tupu as Bialar Crais
Dominique Sweeny as Yoz (movement)
Angie Milliken as of Yoz (voice)
Thomas Holesgrove as Tak (movement)
Nicholas McKay as Tak (voice)
Writer: Michael Cassutt
Director: Ian Watson

SYNOPSIS:

Moya comes across a ship drifting in space. Zhaan takes the transport pod over to check for survivors. Then, suddenly, Moya is attacked by this same ship. As the crew races to get the nicked defense screen from the Zelbinion up and running, a sudden energy pulse from the enemy ship causes some strange things to happen. Rygel, Aeryn and John, in close proximity to each other, come back from momentary unconsciousness to find they've switched bodies. Rygel finds himself in Crichton; Crichton in Aeryn and Aeryn — much to her disgust — finds herself a prisoner in Rygel's body.

Pilot, D'Argo and Chiana have also experienced a body-swapping experience, but here it's more than just inconvenient -- it's deadly. Although a Hynerian's physiology is radically different from either Human or Sebacean, none of these species are engaged in symbiotic relationships. D'Argo, waking up in Pilot's body, is completely overwhelmed by the sudden chaos of impulses, images and sounds from Moya, and Pilot, thrust into the small Nebari, is suddenly cut off from Moya, causing Moya great fear.

On the damaged ship, at first, all Zhaan sees around her is destruction. But suddenly two creatures rise up and imprison her, claiming another of Moya's kind has attacked them. Reasoning it can only be Talyn and Crais, Zhaan is horrified. She tries to explain that Moya and Talyn are two completely different creatures, but Lord Tak, the commander of the enemy ship, isn't particularly interested in what she has to say. She convinces Lord Tak to examine Moya for himself in order to see Moya is no threat to them. Zhaan stays behind with Lord Tak's companion, Yoz, as hostage and Lord Tak arrives on Moya.

During the time Zhaan is in initial negotiations, the six others are desperately trying to figure out how to regain their own bodies and adapt to the ones they find themselves in. Rygel, in Crichton's body, must figure out how to relieve himself moments before Tak arrives and is practically still zipping up when the doors open.

Touring the ship, Tak vomits in one of the hallways. Later the crew discover that his regurgitation is actually an acid which seriously inhibits the defense screen's operation.

On the Halosian (this is a phoenetic approximation for the spelling of this word) ship, Yoz admits to Zhaan that Tak is simply trying to move up through the ranks, and he fired first upon Talyn. Realizing that Talyn was only responding in self-defense sets Zhaan's mind at ease about the leviathan offspring. But this truth only makes their situation more dangerous as it is clear that Tak will attack Moya again in order to increase his number of hostile kills. Yoz says the only way she can remove him from command is to prove that he has failed in his attempted attack on Moya.

Tak returns. A second burst from his energy weapon sends the crew into new bodies again. This time Rygel ends up in Aeryn's body; Aeryn finds herself in Crichton and Crichton is dumped into the Hynerial royal. Pilot, D'Argo and Chiana are also bounced again and it becomes clear that, for some reason, Nebari physiology is unable to withstand a mind/body split. Chiana's body is close to death. Chiana's consciousness, now in Pilot's body, is unable to make sense of any of Moya's signals and because her own body is becoming unresponsive, Pilot cannot communicate with her.

Working together, the crew finally realizes that they must get the defense screen up to sixty-five percent. A final energy burst from the enemy ship will set things right. But Zhaan, having finally convinced Yoz to overthrow the Tak after his second attack on Moya "fails" is more than a little distressed when commanded to fire upon her crewmates for a third time.

She acquiesces finally, and everyone is restored to their respective bodies.

CRITIQUE:

If you've ever wondered what happened to the bad guys in Henson's production of Dark Crystal, wonder no more. Looking a bit worse for wear having been warehoused for all these years, Henson rolls out the strange and frightening nasties to live another incarnation as Halosians. Fans of Dark Crystal will note the similarity in speech patterns and vocal inflection. Here, too, is the basic plot device of an "underling" who has a better moral code (theoretically, in this case) working to overthrow a corrupt ruler. Additionally, both races kill the same way.

As we have seen several times in this season, Zhaan is once again separated from the crew. Here, she must use all her powers as a negotiator and a representative of the peaceful solution to convince Yoz — since Tak seems beyond redemption — that killing her helpless crewmates is not appropriate. Although it's nice to see Ms. Hey holding her own in these kind of scenarios, I personally miss the way she interacts with the others. The lovers' pairings John/Aeryn and, by the end of this episode, Chiana/D'Argo leaves Zhaan largely out of the loop, the proverbial fifth wheel. Rygel and Pilot have always been outsiders to some degree. We know that Rygel is not a "body breeder" and Moya is hermaphroditic. Pilot, because of his relationship with Moya is obviously not looking for a mate — physically or emotionally. Although I am extraordinarily pleased with the way Chiana's addition to the crew has reshaped the dynamics, I worry that Zhaan will get short shrift in the long run.

There is really a lot to like in this episode and it's obvious everyone has a wonderful time exploring the other characters. Mr. Browder is dead-on in his vocal and body work both as Aeryn and Rygel. His depth as an actor really shows here as he's allowed to stretch. John Crichton, by necessity (see critique of "Premiere" in the first volume of these guides) is archetypal and although there is always some leeway within the archetype, the basic guidelines of the character are pretty narrow.

By the same token, watching Ms. Black cut loose during the time when Aeryn is "possessed" by John is one of the two most erotically charged scenes. Although watching Aeryn do the "shimmy" is comic, watching "John" put his hand inside Aeryn's vest is ... well. As Crichton says in his notes (see the scifi channel's Farscape site for his take on this experience), for a man to experience having breasts is reason enough to stay locked in the privacy of one's room forever.

The other wonderful comic/erotic sequence involves Chiana in D'Argo's body and Rygel in John's. Chiana wants to flee and tries to convince Rygel that Crichton's body offers more than the usual Hynerian pleasures to explore. One well-placed hand is enough to give Rygel/John pause, but ultimately the Hynerian knows the only way for him to regain the throne is to overthrow his cousin — but to do that, he must be in his own body. Killing his cousin, he admits at one point during this episode, is all that he lives for.

For the would-be lovers, the experience of being in the other's body is an almost inevitable step in their exploration of their relationship. For D'Argo and Chiana, this experience allows them to open to the potential of being together. For John and Aeryn, it seems more playful and the way they tease each other at the episode's end shows the closeness they all too rarely share.

For Pilot, he's had another incredible experience. In "The Way We Weren't," he tells Valorek that all he ever dreamed about was seeing the stars. For him, being bonded to Moya resulted in a joyful union. But to have experienced the mobility of a biped was also extraordinary.

Some of the questions this episode raises have to do with Pilot's symbiotic relationship with Moya. As we saw in "The Way We Weren't," the pilot will die if separated from the leviathan after joining. But here, there is another consciousness in Pilot's body and yet both Pilot and Chiana are in mortal danger during the course of these events. Is it Nebari physiology that rejects a host consciousness? Is Nebari physiology not as evolved in some way? Does another consciousness overwhelm them? Does Pilot's consciousness have to be in his body for him to survive? For Moya to survive? Although Pilot is able to explain to D'Argo how to listen to the information Moya is transmitting, D'Argo struggles with the multi-tasking. Writer Michael Cassutt does a wonderful job here describing the different messages in terms of sound and color. Seeing into Pilot/Moya is an incredible experience and one we'll get a bit more of in the three-part "Look at the Princess" arc.

The sets and lighting in this episode are also great, especially on Lord Tak's ship. Be sure not to miss the silhouette of Zhaan's lovely feminine shape ;) But I could have done without the green teeth lighting.

Finally, kudos to Gus Gross. The subtle use of sound and music, especially in the scene where D'Argo begins to comprehend the intricate harmony between Moya and Pilot is very well done.

A solid episode, light-hearted and fun but with some depth and purpose.

Grade: A

Episode 10212: My Three Crichtons
Location: Uncharted Territories
Writer: Gabrielle Stanton & Harry Werksman, Jr
Director: Catherine Millar

SYNOPSIS:

When a tiny sphere of "light" enters Moya, it seems to be looking for something. Hovering over each of the crew in turn, it finally stops directly over Crichton's head. Crichton, panicked, tells Aeryn to shoot it. She fires and the light engulfs Crichton completely.

A few moments later, Crichton is flung back out, closely followed by a hairy ape-like beast that flees immediately. Although everyone looks for the creature, it is Chiana who finds him in Crichton's quarters, struggling to clothe himself in Crichton's IASA uniform. Though his speech is garbled, Chaina quickly realizes that this creature is John Crichton -- although it seems as though it's either a completely separate entity or some part of Crichton that has been separated from his original form.

A DNA scan confirms that this new arrival is indeed Crichton, but the crew is soon consumed by a new crisis: The sphere is creating energy fluctuations which, left unresolved, will eventually tear the leviathan apart.

During one extremely powerful fluxuation, out pops another version of Crichton, completely naked, covered only by whispy shreds of mist. As startling as the hairy version of Crichton was, this one is even stranger: He not only has a larger head, no hair and smaller ears, but he's missing ... something the original Crichton values quite a bit.

It quickly becomes clear that this Crichton is an evolved version of the Original. Smarter, calmer, more reserved and -- ultimately -- more emotionally cold. As if one Crichton weren't enough, now there are three. And Pilot informs the crew that if they don't do something about the energy fluctuations, they'll all be pulled into another dimension.

When the crew realizes that the sphere won't depart without one of the Crichtons for its scientific sample bag, it seems pretty clear which one will be sacrificed — the Neanderthal Crichton. Chiana, however, has become fiercely protective of this version as it encapsulates everything she loves about John. Neanderthal Crichton is a wholly emotional being as much as Evolved Crichton is wholly intellectual. Chiana releases Neanderthal Crichton from the holding cell and Original Crichton manages to find him by knowing instinctually where he would hide. In the end, Neanderthal Crichton bests Evolved Crichton in a brawl and disappears with him into the sphere. The sphere withdraws moments before Moya would have been ripped out of her dimension and thrust into another one.

CRITIQUE:

Another familiar scifi plot gets re-worked here with mostly positive results. Star Trek plummed the depths of splitting psyches in the original series as well as in The Next Generation. From the split-personality Kirk in "The Enemy Within" to the alternate universe scenario in TOS' "Mirror, Mirror" and the oft-visited alternate universe in Deep Space Nine, there has always been a fascination with what makes us who we are.

Once it becomes clear that Crichton has not been split into three different parts of the whole which have to be reunited to survive, the plot and its outcome were obvious. The problem with this basic story is that the writers are working with archetypes which are very limited. Neanderthal Crichton has to be emotional, frightened, gentle, aggressive and unable to communicate except through grunts and a garbled version of Original John's understanding of speech. In the same way, Evolved Crichton has to be emotionally cold and intellectual with flawless logic and reasoning. He has grown beyond the needs of his physical body and the loss of his gender (not just the physical attributes that determine sex). Given these restrictions, pairing Neanderthal Crichton with child-like Chiana and Evolved Crichton with emotionally-aloof Aeryn makes sense. The D'Argo/Original Crichton combination of two "regular guys" working together reinforces this triad.

Because of these archetypes, the story here isn't really very interesting. Obviously, the others will choose to "sacrifice" the less evolved creature. The Original Crichton and the Evolved Crichton both offer something to the crew. But what does Neanderthal Crichton have to offer a space-faring, technological society?

Notice, too, how the costuming choices underscore these three aspects of Crichton. Neanderthal Crichton dons John's original uniform — reminding us that he belongs to another time and place. Original Crichton wears his everyday clothing which shows us how he's grown and adapted to this new world. Evolved Crichton wears the red leather PK lieutenant's attire underlining the attitude of PK superiority which Aeryn remarks upon from time to time.

However, digging deeper into the thematic meanings below the simple plot does uncover some disturbing evidence. The story asks us to consider what makes a life valuable. It asks us to put a value on a sentient individual's life. As with "DNA Mad Scientist," it raises questions about ethics and morality in science. Who — and what — has the right to survive? And who is equipped to make those decisions?

While Zhaan struggles with the idea of having to make any compromise that will endanger any of the Crichtons while also protecting her shipmates and Moya, Evolved Crichton chides her for wasting time mulling over a decision that is, for him, crystal clear.

Aeryn finds Evolved Crichton distasteful and even cruel — a good choice. Perhaps Aeryn will see the coldness in Evolved Crichton and make the connection between his aloof personality and the part of herself that's afraid to be connected to anyone else. Maybe even seeing Neanderthal Crichton will help her let go and let someone inside her protective circle.

Chiana's ability to comfort and draw out Neanderthal Crichton adds another dimension to the Crichton/Chiana relationship and really lets us see a softer side of a character who has endured some incredibly difficult experiences and is usually willing to go a lot further than the rest of the crew to survive.

Mr. Browder is excellent in all three versions of his character. What a treat to see him stretch. And what an interesting take on evolution: Creation, in this version of the story, is the by-product of genetic research. A kind of scientific afterthought rather than the deliberate and delicate handiwork of God.

Grade: B

Episode 10210: Look at the Princess Part 1: A Kiss is But a Kiss
Location: The Royal Planet
Guest Cast:
Matt Day as Tyno
Wayne Pygram as Scorpius
Tina Bursill as Novia
Felix Williamson as Prince Clavor
Felicity Price as Princess Katralla
Bianca Chiminello as Jena
Aaron Cash as Dregon
Gavin RObins as Cargn
Jonathan Hardy as Kahaynu
Francesca Buller as ro-NA
Writer: David Kemper
Director: Andrew Proses and Tony Tilse

SYNOPSIS:

"A Kiss is But a Kiss" is the first of a three-episode classic scifi story arc. In the tradition of a sprawling epic, writer David Kemper separates the crew and jumps back and forth among a number of different storylines.

The setup for much of what happens, especially between Aeryn and John, begins when they're inside the cockpit of Farscape 1. John notices Aeryn's hair smells nice; she's pleased he's noticed; they kiss. They kiss some more and then suddenly Aeryn blows the hatch and jumps out. Crichton, understandably confused and upset, reminds her that she's the one who started it, even though she's blaming him.

A short time later, Moya encounters a deadly field of space-mines. Defenseless, Zhaan and the others plead for mercy and are granted leave to visit the Royal Planet, despite the high security measures surrounding preparations for a coronation. But who will rule is still very much in question. Crichton, Aeryn, D'Argo, Chiana and Rygel take a transport pod planetside. There, Crichton is overjoyed to find that all the girls want to kiss him after first placing a drop of some sort of liquid on his tongue. Aeryn, though pleased to be surrounded by Sebaceans again, is disgusted by Crichton's behavior and retreats behind a shell of caustic sarcasm.

Aeryn receives a dressing down from Chiana who calls her on the mixed messages she's sending Crichton. From Chiana's point of view, it's obvious that Aeryn's attracted to Crichton and vice versa and Chiana reminds Aeryn that men are basically thick-headed and need to be told bluntly what is what. Chiana, as we have seen, is extremely resourceful and more than willing to use her feminine charms to get what she wants, needs or feels will help the crew ("Home on the Remains"). Aeryn, torn between action and the absolute terror of letting her guard down, vacillates back and forth, coming close to telling

John how she feels but then backing away at the last moment.

And Crichton isn't much help either: It seems that he's the only man on the planet — literally — who is genetically compatible with Princess Katralla. He's flattered when she asks him to marry, but really doesn't take the situation too seriously. Unfortunately, everyone else involved is deadly serious — and many of the major political players don't want Katralla to become Empress.

Katralla's strongest opposition is found in her brother, Prince Clavor, a repulsive troll of a man who plays both sides against the middle in an effort to get his way. He's entered into a potentially suicidal pact with a race called the Scarrans. The Scarran Emissary wants to secure the Royal Planet's alliance — something unheard of in their history of Switzerland-like neutrality. Clavor wants power. And he's willing to sacrifice thousands, if not millions, of lives to get it.

The Scarran Emissary has altered Princess Katralla's DNA so that she is incompatible with anyone on the planet. This, of course, is a huge stumbling block as it prevents her from having children who will be healthy enough to rule. And in all of their history, the Emperor and his Consort (or in this case the Empress and hers) are a heterosexual pair of genetically compatible individuals who will produce strong, intelligent offspring fit to take over the responsibility of guiding the planet's government once the current ruler steps down.

Clavor, despite the fact that he's an evil excuse for a Prince, will ascend the throne in Katralla's place if she cannot find a suitable mate. Clavor and his fiancée, Jenavia, are already scheming, as is the Scarran Emissary, about what they'll do once they seize power. When Crichton and Katralla kiss and their compatibility is revealed, Clavor is livid. At the last moment, something has shifted the balance in Katralla's favor.

Meanwhile, back aboard Moya, Zhaan continues in

her spiritual practices, involving both Pilot and Moya in a ritual. But their peace is rudely interrupted by the arrival of a Peacekeeper Command Carrier. And Scorpius. Thinking their best hope of survival is to flee and come back later for those planetside, they break orbit. Shortly thereafter, Moya senses something that she must follow and starbursts toward this calling. The starburst invalidates all previous coordinates, which will make it very difficult for them to return for the others. But soon enough, all three of them are caught up in such incredible beauty that they seem to forget momentarily about the plight of their friends and of their own precarious position. Pilot, after a moment of quiet contemplation, says he believes they are looking upon God — the Builders, the Creators. The ones who created leviathans and brought them into the universe.

Planetside, the current Empress (Katralla and Clavor's mother) draws Crichton aside just before the formal announcement of the wedding. She urges Crichton to marry Katralla, pointing out that a Scarran alliance will destroy everything their people created over centuries of careful and isolated culture building. The Scarran alliance, she tells Crichton, will bring the wrath of the Peacekeepers down on their heads, so volitile is the animosity between the two races. When Crichton hesitates, she plays her trump card: Scorpius. The mere mention of Scorpius' name sends Crichton into a cold sweat.

Crichton wrestles with his conscience. He's so undone and oblivious that he walks right in on D'Argo and Chiana in flagrante delicto — for the second time. This clearly angers Chiana and she stalks off, leaving D'Argo wrapped up like a cute puppy in a quilt, looking like quite the sensitive lover. The two companions have a long heart to heart talk. D'Argo tells Crichton that perhaps marrying Katralla is his destiny. Crichton reminds D'Argo that immediately after the ceremony, both he and Katralla will be turned into living statues — for eighty cycles. By the time they are awakened, everyone Crichton knows will be dead.

Ultimately, however, Crichton's conscience conquers his fear. Or perhaps his fear of being in Scorpius' clutches again is a greater evil than eighty cycles as a bronze bird-perch. He agrees to the wedding and very shortly thereafter is ambushed by four thugs who seem bent on killing him.

CRITIQUE:

Writer/Producer David Kemper draws heavily from a number of sources to create this epic-feeling story arc. At it's heart, Farscape itself is a quest story: A hero (Crichton) searching for a way home. Homer's epic poem, The Odyssey, also traces such a journey, one fraught with danger, intrigue and adventure. But instead of Penelope, it is Jack Crichton who awaits John's return, which is an interesting interweaving of two classic mythology arcs devoted to the hero's adventure: The search for the father and the journey home.

Consider, for example, Luke Skywalker's quest. He spends an enormous amount of time and energy searching for his father only to discover that the father figure he'd created in his imagination was nothing like the reality of Darth Vader. And when Skywalker learns the truth, the first thing he does is run from it. Likewise, when Crichton first learns the truth about his compatibility with Princess Katralla and thus his possible destiny, he denies the inevitable outcome of his actions.

Many cultures use the reluctant hero motif to thrust a kind of everyman (or everywoman) into a strange set of circumstances to see how he or she will react. Crichton is our hero (see discussion of "Premiere" in the Season 1 Episode Guide). And because he's set up as our Odysseus, he must face a number of situations which will test his mettle as a hero before he can be returned to his former life.

This framework is what sets the story in motion. Crichton unknowingly walks into a situation which will change the shape of a world's history. And change his own life as well. Prior to this adventure, he struggles with trying to figure out how to be with Aeryn (getting angry despite what he learned about her in "The Way We Weren't"), watching two of his shipmates couple-up, cope with extreme emotional, spiritual, psychic (and possibly physical) damage done him by Scorpius. He has a complex, rich life stranger and in some ways more wonderful than he ever imagined. Propelled into this world by an unanticipated event, which in this case was the creation of the wormhole during his experiement (and in Skywalker's case was the murder of his aunt and uncle), he has no choice but to survive or perish.

Most of the first episode is given to setting up the complex set of circumstances which are changed by Crichton's arrival and the fact of his genetic compatibility. The Clavor/Scarran alliance and the Empress' concern that her son's disposition and desire for power beyond his need will destroy a world she has protected and served for many cycles are the major plot elements of this first section.

Additionally, the changing relationships among the crew members have to be redefined and explored. First, D'Argo and Chiana have acted on their attraction and their focus has turned primarily toward each other. This seems to annoy everyone at some point and in different ways.

For Aeryn, it seems one more way in which she sees herself as separate from Chiana. Chiana is willing to take a chance and follow her heart. She's willing to be hurt and disappointed, but also willing to experience the emotional joy and physical ecstasy that sexual intimacy with D'Argo brings. Aeryn is, at this point, willing to take neither risk. She continually rebuffs Dregon, a handsome would-be suitor who bluntly offers to take Aeryn's mind off her troubles. And she brushes off Chiana's down-to-earth advice about dealing with men.

Chiana is right when she says she knows the opposite sex. She has clearly demonstrated an ability to appeal to, manipulate and cajole in order to get what she wants or needs. Interestingly enough, her relationship with D'Argo seems more about the heart than about the outcome. If she wants something specific from him other than his love and companionship, it's not obvious.

D'Argo confides his feelings for Chiana to John and pleads with Crichton not to screw things up. For all his male posturing, this seems to indicate that D'Argo is not so self-assured as he would like everyone to believe — whether it's about his attractiveness to Chiana or his ability to "compete" with Crichton for women. A similar competitiveness rose once before in "Back and Back and Back to the Future" with Matala who was openly flirting with D'Argo, but sending sexually explicit images to John.

John and Aeryn, as a couple, can't seem to decide how to proceed. I can certainly empathize with Crichton's feelings that he's being given mixed messages, but it's just as clear that every time Aeryn takes one step forward, she is overwhelmed by her fears and panics. Unfortunately, this push-pull aspect of her personality is pretty much all she's allowed to explore during this three-part story. Each time she gathers her courage to approach Crichton, he is unable to respond to the subtext of her message. When she urges him to flee, as they have always done, he disabuses her of the notion that it will work. His own mental gyrations about what is right versus what he wants are so uppermost in his thoughts that he can't really see what Aeryn is proposing.

So in the first part, we see a lot of missed messages, mixed messages and blown opportunities for the two of them to talk honestly and openly about their feelings.

And then we have Zhaan, Pilot and Moya. Separating them from most of the crew was risky, but ultimately this separate storyline will pay off. The beauty of the ritual, Zhaan's singing resonating within Moya are both wonderful spiritual moments. And their storyline only gets better.

What doesn't work in this first of three episodes is mostly minor. Zhaan's comment that she's surprised there are Sebacean colonies this far into the Uncharted Territories seems odd given Moya's recent proximity to the Gammak base. The Gammak base was hidden deep in the Territories, and yet quite populated. What would seem odd about a Sebacean colony this far removed? The Uncharted Territories are clearly very inhabited. And the only ones who don't have charts are Moya and her crew. Everyone else seems to be able to get around just fine.

Additionally, if the translator microbes can translate all words which have compatible words or phrases, why do words like "dren," and "frell" for example, not come through in English? Although the answer to this part of the question is obvious (the censors won't permit offensive language in a PG-13 show), why do we hear "microt," "metre," and "arn" instead of their English counterparts? Does John hear the others speak in their native languages and then gets the translation a moment later? Do the other seem to speak their own languages but he hears them in English (think badly dubbed foreign film)? Just a thought.

When Crichton interrupts D'Argo and Chiana for the second time as they're having sex, listen to D'Argo's footfalls when he gets up and walks to Crichton during that same scene. He's wearing his boots. Maybe he is just an old space cowboy after all ;).

Why does Moya's starburst nullify all previous coordinates? That seems terribly inconvenient. Does that mean that it's impossible to return to where ever you've been or does that just mean it's hard to figure out? This seemed like a stupid plot trick to make it seem as though Moya, Zhaan and Pilot are really more "lost" than they originally think. And then how was Moya able to reunite with the others in this season's opening episodes? Finally,

do my ears deceive me or does Crichton not say that he's
going to spend sixty cycles as a statue when he's talking to
D'Argo. Earlier, he'd said it was eighty.

Grade: B+

**Episode 10211: Look at the Princess Part 2:
I Do, I Think**
Location: The Royal Planet
Guest Cast:
Matt Day as Tyno
Wayne Pygram as Scorpius
Tina Bursill as Novia
Felix Williamson as Prince Clavor
Felicity Price as Princess Katralla
Bianca Chiminello as Jena
Aaron Cash as Dregon
Gavin RObins as Cargn
Jonathan Hardy as Kahaynu
Francesca Buller as ro-NA
Writer: David Kemper
Director: Andrew Prowse and Tony Tilse

SYNOPSIS:

Clavor's thugs have just about destroed Katralla's
wedding plans and Crichton with them when Crichton is
rescued by an unexpected ally — Jena (Jenavia), Prince
Clavor's fiancée. It turns out that she is actually a
Peacekeeper Disrupter, Special Directory, and it's her job
to make sure that Clavor does not ascend the throne.
Surprised and a bit baffled by the sudden turn of events,
Crichton gathers his wits and wastes no time in confronting
Clavor. The Prince whimpers and denies and is interrupted
by Katralla who storms into the room, slaps Crichton and
demands to talk with him privately.

Katralla's people, she reminds him, are peaceful
and do not go about striking others (even though she just

slapped him) or accusing each other of attempted murder. While Crichton tries to defend himself, their conversation is interrupted by the appearance of a strange globe hanging in the air. Katralla doesn't know what it is and Crichton is becoming more than a little suspicious. Suddenly, the room fills with smoke. Just as they think they'll succumb, two glowing red orbs appear in the mist. It's ro-NA, and she leads them to safety.

Although D'Argo and Chiana have made no headway convincing the Empress that Crichton needs more protection, Rygel has managed to work out a mutually satisfactory deal which involves getting Crichton off the planet until just before the wedding, thus insuring his safety. They agree to send Crichton to hide on an orbiting freighter filled with wedding presents from ro-NA's people. What they don't know is that Scorpius has bribed ro-NA into giving Crichton a different trans-sequence ident wafer which will not, as she tells Crichton, hide their position, but broadcast their position to Scorpius instead.

He realizes that ro-NA has sold him out when Lieutenant Braca, weapon in hand, and informs Crichton he's going to be taken prisoner. When ro-NA contacts Scorpius to tell him everything is under control, Scorpius instructs Braca to make sure that ro-NA receives her "reward" and Crichton arrives unharmed as his brain is "unique."

This is all Crichton needs to hear. Unwilling to become Scorpius' prisoner again, Crichton starts pushing buttons on the console, knowing the Lieutenant won't shoot him and thus turns Scorpius' rage upon the Lieutenant. Crichton activates the weapons' array which starts firing at the planetary defense system satellites. Both the Lieutenant and ro-NA are killed as Crichton rails against his enemies and his fate. Then, in a moment of inspiration, Crichton decides he'll blow himself out the hatch and use a pulse rifle to propel himself from the freighter to the transport pod, which is a short distance away. Moments after he enters the vacuum of space, the defense satellites destroy the freighter. Crichton manages to enter the transport pod and return to the planet's surface.

Recovering in his room, he and D'Argo have a final heart-to-heart talk. Then, in a fantastic and elaborate, but blessedly short wedding ceremony, Crichton is wedded to the Princess. D'Argo, Chiana and Rygel all wish him well. Shortly thereafter, the Princess ascends to the platform where the statue-making will commence and becomes a bronzed version of herself. Crichton steps into his place beside her. Tyno, Katralla's lover and would-be husband, apologizes to Crichton in advance, telling him that the bronzing machine is calibrated for Sebaceans and that his experience is going to be painful. D'Argo gets a final laugh out of Crichton by telling him that the good news is that D'Argo and Chiana are if not genetically, at least sexually compatible. The machine whirs; Crichton screams. Moments later, he's the Farscape equivalent of Han Solo after he's been frozen by Baba Fett.

Throughout this entire sequence, Aeryn vacillates between telling Crichton she loves him and telling him to go stuff himself. She comes to see him one last time before the ceremony and implores him to run away. Exhausted by the multiple attempts on his life and feeling trapped by his limited choices, he lies down on his bed, puts a pillow under his head and essentially tells her he's had enough. He's not going to fight any more.

Furious, both with Crichton and her inability to convince him to leave, Aeryn storms out of the palace, passing Dregon on the way. She tells him that she's going climbing and that if he wants to accompany her .... He can barely shed his formal robes fast enough to follow her and they head for the rocky coast. Although Crichton looks for her at the wedding, he is not surprised to find her absent.

During this time, Zhaan and Pilot have had their own adventures. The Builders, it seems, are not benevolent creators. They send their representative, Kahaynu to inform Pilot and Moya that Moya's life will be terminated because she has birthed a leviathan-gunship hybrid.

Zhaan, completely outraged, argues nobly on Moya's behalf, but Kahaynu will not be persuaded. At the end of this segment of the three-episode arc, Zhaan and Pilot say their goodbyes as Moya is systematically shut down.

CRITIQUE:

"I Do, I Think" suffers too much from storytelling's middle-child syndrome. There's too much emphasis on making sure everyone who missed last week's episode will be able to follow the plot resulting in a middle section that drags terribly. As a writer, Kemper needs to be more judicious with his editing. He needs to remember that story he's trying to tell and not allow himself to get sidetracked by reminding us about what has gone before. That's what the little trailer during the opening teaser is for.

Perhaps he should look to American novelist John Irving whose screenplay for The Cider House Rules won an Academy Award. In one of the only successful translations from novel to screen, Irving managed to compress his own complex novel with many different plots, themes and characters into a movie which was focused, fully realized and short enough to ensure a successful theatrical run. As a writer, Kemper could learn a lot from this man. He should also pick up a copy of Robert McKee's Story, which is probably the best book about writing for the screen available. In a three-episode arc like this one, Kemper is essentially writing a full-length film, even though he has less work to do in terms of introducing and developing characters. But he tends to be repetitive and lazy, which essentially ruins any chance his writing has for being anything other than average.

For example, most of the Scarran-Clavor alliance is reexamined almost verbatim. Aeryn and Chiana have a conversation which pretty much reiterates everything Chiana said in "A Kiss is But a Kiss." Every conversation Aeryn and John have follows the same pattern and does not move the story forward in any way. It's just filler and should have been edited out. Perhaps Kemper should have made this a two-episode story rather than a three-episode one.

Additionally, there's the problem of ro-NA's people. She says that they are not allowed to acquire wealth. This would account for her desire for a material reward to betray Crichton, but doesn't account for the fact that there's a ship full of presents from ro-NA's people in orbit around the planet. If they don't acquire wealth, why are they sending material gifts? And if there's a difference between wealth and material gifts, why wasn't it made more distinct in the script?

Additionally ro-NA's people seem to be a slave race — a serving race. Why would they send gifts? How could they send gifts? And the Empress, who does not seem like a fool, is so convinced of ro-NA's loyalty that she would trust her life to her. And ro-NA does not hesitate to betray her. Not being willing to acknowledge and take action against a devastating character flaw in one's own child (namely Clavor) is one thing, but having been a statute for eighty cycles (observing and learning about culture and government) and then having ruled for twenty or so more, she seems strangely naive about some very basic tenet of government: A ruling class and a serving class are certain to come to blows, despite the best and most peaceful intentions. Huge disparities in wealth and power always lead to resentment, anger and finally violence. Look at a hundred years in any culture and you will see this happen time and again. The Empress is such a shrewd negotiator, especially in the outstanding scenes with Rygel, that these slips really stick out.

And for someone who's been around palace politics for a while, ro-NA seems a little too naive. The fact that she never questioned Scorpius' motives, never suspected that her life would be forfeit since she would know what happened to the much-coveted Crichton just doesn't ring true. Kemper needs to spend more time looking into psychology and the way class, money and power affect one's desires, perceptions and behaviors. In the end, ro-NA doesn't really get the depth she deserves, an aspect that could have been easily addressed by a more perceptive observer of human nature.

Although scifi is often considered a genre for geeks and social outcasts, the best scifi writers are great observers of humanity and inspired open-minded thinkers. They make connections between disparit parts, fitting them together to make something never seen before. They open up worlds and galaxies where we as readers and viewers can come to be entertained and enlightened. But across the board, no matter what the genre, good writing is good writing. And as Robert McKee stresses in his book, the story is the most important part. The reason stories like The Iliad and The Odyssey and Beowulf have survived for centuries is not just because they're on required reading lists in many in educational institutions. It's because they're good stories with engaging characters. If they weren't, present-day writers (not to mention canonical writers such as Shakespeare or Dickens), would not continue to openly borrow from the best of our literature to create modern-day heroes. The characters, their background and their actions have to be believable, fully-realized, three-dimensional. And this means a writer has to take the time to do his or her homework — whether it's studying psychology, history, science of whatever. A writer is responsible for knowing everything about the world and the people she or he creates. And only at that point, should we enter the writer's vision of that world.

Speaking of research, there has been much

discussion about Crichton's space walk. Many contemporary films including Black Hole and Mission to Mars have scenes which include a human being exposed to the vacuum of space. In Black Hole, the character implodes. In Mission to Mars, the astronaut removes his helmet and is immediately frozen solid. Unfortunately, both of these depictions are incorrect. Kemper comes believably close to the scientific reality.

While it is certainly not recommended that one take off the proscribed protective clothing while in between the stars, according to the NASA website (which is quite fascinating and worth a visit) this is what would happen:

Exposing a human body to a vacuum would not cause permanent damage if the following conditions were met. First, that the exposure was relatively short. In an incident at the Johnson Space Center in 1965, a subject was accidentally exposed to near vacuum conditions when his space suit was defective and was leaking. After fourteen seconds, the man lost consciousness as this is roughly the amount of time it took for the oxygen left in his system to be consumed -- or to see it another way, for the oxygen-deprived blood to get to his brain. Although the man was not exposed to what's called a "hard vacuum" as Crichton was, he was revived. The last thing he remembered before blacking out was that the saliva on his tongue was beginning to boil.

A second incident occurred during an open-gondola flight in 1965 when Joe Kittinger lost pressure in his right hand glove. He was flying at 19.5 miles above the Earth. The hand became numb and useless, but returned to normal functioning once he returned to ground level.

Space, like the ocean, will wreak havoc on an astronaut's Eustachian tubes (the tube that connects your inner ear to the back of your throat). Many people have experienced this very thing when ascending in an airplane — that uncomfortable feeling of your ears "popping." As with diving, this is the body's way of trying to equalize the pressure on either side of the eardrum. This is why divers are careful to ascend slowly from great depths. A rapid ascent will cause the bends, a condition in which gasses trapped in the tissues are released when a subject moves from a compressed atmosphere to a decompressed one, causing neuralgic pain, paralysis, difficulty breathing and in some cases death. If Crichton had expelled the oxygen in his lungs before entering space, he would survive for longer as he wouldn't risk severe damage to his lungs right off.

He would probably lose consciousness in about fifteen seconds, though, as soon as his oxygen supply ran out. How long this would take is not known at this point, but according to the specialists at NASA, death be imminent within two minutes. During this exposure, one could also acquire a nasty sunburn and some minor swelling of the tissues beneath the skin. It is, therefore, possible for Crichton to have survived his little spacewalk from the freighter to the transport pod.

One's blood does not boil and explosion (or implosion) are not immediate because of containing factors of both the circulatory system and the skin. And although no one will argue that the vacuum of space is extraordinarily cold, you would not immediately become a human freeze-pop since it would take some time for the heat to transfer away from your body.

In this, Kemper has checked out the hard science behind the scene.

More than anyone else in this storyline, Crichton goes through is dark night of the soul. When he realizes that he's important enough to Scorpius that Braca won't risk harming him, he shifts into a manic what-have-I-got-to-live-for mode that's takes not only Braca, but also the viewers by surprise. In an Internet chat, Kemper revealed that some of Crichton's monologue there was improvised "on the floor" as the set is called, especially the bits about Braca destroying Crichton's sex life by shooting him in the hand.

The fact that Braca doesn't understand Human physiology enough to realize any major injury to Crichton will result in death gives John the edge he needs. Until the very end, it seems that Crichton has chosen death over possible rescue and possibly becoming Scorpius' prisoner again. When Crichton realizes he'd rather die than face the Aurora Chair — or another form of this torture — viewers are given a powerful reminder of just how devastating that experience was for John. He's not just telling stories when he tells Aeryn how much Scorpius scares him.

In the end, Crichton proves that he's an honorable man in terms of the big picture. Instead of choosing himself, he chooses to try and protect and preserve a planet whose culture is worth saving. He chooses the difficult road, the one which is perhaps his destiny, knowing that to say yes to this is to say no to Aeryn, his friends and crewmates and any hope of returning to Earth.

Certainly this is not an easy decision to make, nor should it be. The hero must face his demons and his fears in order to be victorious. And that is precisely what Crichton is trying to do.

The Pilot-Zhaan-Moya storyline takes a fascinating turn here. Kahaynu (a version of the Big Kahuna, perhaps?) turns out to be even worse than expected. Despite Zhaan's pleas, he sentences Moya — and therefore Pilot and Zhaan — to death. In a beautifully rendered scene between Pilot and Zhaan, they comfort each other as death reaches for them and we are truly left to wonder whether or not this will be the end of this particular part of the storyline (although we suspect that it is not). And one final note for the fan-addict ... Kahaynu is played by Jonathan Hardy, the fellow who provides the voice for Rygel.

Grade: C

Episode 10211: Look at the Princess Part 3:
The Maltese Crichton
Location: The Royal Planet
Guest Cast:
Matt Day as Tyno
Wayne Pygram as Scorpius
Tina Bursill as Novia
Felix Williamson as Prince Clavor
Felicity Price as Princess Katralla
Bianca Chiminello as Jena
Aaron Cash as Dregon
Gavin RObins as Cargn
Jonathan Hardy as Kahaynu
Francesca Buller as ro-NA
Writer: David Kemper
Director: Andrew Prowse and Tony Tilse

SYNOPSIS:

In the Crichton story arc, this final installment opens with Crichton and Katralla standing in a now-empty hall. D'Argo and Chiana come to visit him and through the use of a translating device, say their final goodbyes. Shortly thereafter, some wicked person enters the hall and whacks Crichton's head off. We find out moments later that Prince Clavor and the Scarran emissary are still determined to place Clavor on the throne. So they throw Crichton's head into a pool of acid.

But luckily for Crichton, Scorpious rescues the head, probalby with the intent of cracking it open and sucking out the secrets of the wormhole technology. (A nod here to the Borg Queen in Star Trek: Voyager's episode "Unimatrix Zero" who uses a nasty mind probe to try and discover who among the collective has managed to retain their individuality.)

Crichton gets even luckier when Jena comes to his head's rescue and manages to wrest it away from

Scorpious. She reattaches his head to his body and then un-bronzes him. (And thus the Star Wars / Han Solo plot aspect of this trilogy is complete.) They escape to her fully-equipped (but somehow totally hidden high tech) camp somewhere in the hills. She demands he tell her the real truth. He says she won't believe him, but cooperates. Then they have sex in a lake and do their pillow talk wrapped in a giant blanket on a rock. Jena gives him a weapon disguised to look like an ugly necklace. They agree to meet again in the palace in the morning.

Meanwhile, Dregon and Aeryn are half-way up a challenging rock face when Dregon freezes. Despite Aeryn's attempts to help him move past his fear, he panics, grabs at her leg, pulls her off balance and they both go crashing into the rock-filled water below. Both survive, though Aeryn has broken her leg and Dregon is unable to stand.

On Moya, Zhaan gets fed up with Kahaynu and sucks him into one of the prowler's engines. Just when we think he's dead, he reappears (not unlike Dracula) and then tells Zhaan that this has all been an elaborate test to see whether or not she would be willing to sacrifice everything, including her own life, to protect Moya from anyone who would try and hurt her.

Back on the Royal Planet, the Scarran emissary captures Chiana after D'Argo unwittingly mentions that she might know where Crichton is hiding. We find out that the Scarran believes there will be a war between the Scarrans and the Peacekeepers. D'Argo and Scorpius become uncomfortable allies in the search for Chiana.

Prince Clavor and the Scarran meet together in the garden. Clavor finally pushes the Scarran too far and the emissary kills him. This leads to the Empress declaring that not only will no off-worlders be allowed to leave the planet, but that they'll all be put to death, which really upsets Rygel in particular.

Crichton returns to the palace and hooks up with

Jena who says she's walking funny this morning -- and it's not from the hiking they did the day before. D'Argo and Scorpius walk into the Scarran's trap. It seems he's used Chiana as bait to lure both the Luxan and Scorpius into a situation where he could eliminate them. The Scarran believes that Scorpius is somehow involved in the complex politics on this planet and in the struggle for control over a world which has refused all alliances.

Scorpius finally manages to convince the Scarran that he has no allegiences to anyone but himself -- his interest is purely in John Crichton. About this time, Crichton arrives and using the necklace weapon given him by Jena, manages to kill the Scarran. During the scuffle, one of the chains holding Chiana over the vat of acid breaks and as the second one snaps, D'Argo lauches himself through the air saving Chiana at the last possible moment.

The Scarran falls into the acid vat. Crichton pushes Scorpius to the very edge of the vat, holding his face inches from the bubbling pool. But he can't push him in. He can't kill him. In a moment of human compassion — or perhaps frailty — Crichton tells Scorpius to leave him alone and stalks off.

In the statue room, Crichton conferences with the Empress, Tyno and Katralla. When Crichton finds out that Katralla is pregnant with his child, he heroically volunteers to become a statue again (despite his unfaithfullness of the night before). In the end, however, Tyno steps up and agrees not only to serve as Katralla's consort, but also to raise Crichton's child as his own. Crichton is gifted with a moment with a hologram of his unborn daughter.

Everyone agrees that they will simply rewrite history and pretend that Crichton never happened. One only hopes they've got some extra DNA samples stored away for subsequent offspring. The Empress has decided to spare all their lives.

Crichton and the others return to Moya.

In the final scene, we return again to the hanger deck where this all began. Aeryn produces a vial of the compatability liquid. Crichton agrees to taste it. They kiss. Aeryn turns away from Crichton and smiles.

CRITIQUE:

In general, this was not a very satisfying resolution to this story. Although Kemper started off strong, he began to falter in the second part and really stumbles in this third installment. The problems overshadow what does work here, unfortunately.

For example, if Katralla can see and hear everything, why can't she tell anyone who lobbed off Crichton's head? She was, after all, standing right there. This leads directly into the laughable conclusion to the Crichton story arc. Crichton mentions several times that he's donated DNA samples. And initially, he asks whether or not all they need from him is a donation to the sperm bank. Raising this question in the first part puts it in our minds but using it as the basic resolution is ridiculous.

Why didn't anyone think of this before? Why didn't the Empress and the Princess just get together and put out a story saying that they had found a suitable donor and that his sperm would be not only used to impregnate the Princess, but also to create future children. With Clavor out of the way, there really is no reason not to go this route. Why didn't they come back and say that the tests had been incorrect and that the Princess actually was compatible with her lover, Tyno, but they had kept it under wraps in order to expose Clavor's evil plot. How can they have such unbelievable technology that allows someone to see their offspring before they're even conceived and get frozen for eighty cycles but can't manage to reverse the DNA changes the Scarran made? By the end of the episode, a classic deus ex machina scene would have been more believable than what we got.

The Empress' speech about making sure that their solution didn't leave that room was just plain stupid. I'm sorry, but didn't we just see a wedding in the last episode. A wedding with many guests? And what about that initial bar scene where everyone stops to look at Crichton and Katralla after she declares they're compatible? Keeping this a secret is ludicrous. I was stunned that this was the ending the creative team chose to shoot.

And what about these film-referencing titles? Are we supposed to now think of Crichton and Katralla in that "We'll always have Paris" nostalgia? As far as I know, they didn't even have a relationship, much less one with such depth as the one portrayed in Casablanca. The Maltese Falcon had treasure hidden inside of it. Is the treasure hidden inside Crichton's wormhole technology? Or was this just kind of a bad pun about the fact that he was turned into a statue? Calling the cycle "Look at the Princess" doesn't make much sense. I'm looking. Now what? It's not very descriptive. Someone should help Kemper with titles.

Why did John's head float in the acid? It's made out of bronze or some kind of metal, right? Why didn't it sink to the bottom of the pool? At the very least, John's skull wouldn't have floated. A head weighs around twenty pounds. What kind of acid was that anyway? Carbonated acid? And speaking of acid, why wasn't the Scarran immediately dissolved? Does he have an exoskeleton? Or was it just his lizard-like exterior? Why didn't he scream more when his eyeballs were burned out, for example. I mean, if you're going to dissolve someone in acid, you might as well do it right.

Although Crichton had wonderful moments with the three children presented during the story arc and Kemper has gone to great pains to make Crichton out as the noble martyr, as soon as his head and body are reunited, he has sex with Jena. He's willing to be turned into a statue when he finds out Katralla is pregnant with his child, but he is unfaithful to her within the first two days. Perhaps the point here was that Crichton felt he couldn't convince Jena to help him unless he showed her a good time. According to the synopsis on the official scifi channel website (from Crichton's point of view), he glosses over it as a guy thing. Right. It's a guy thing to cheat on your wife within the first forty-eight hours of marriage. It's a guy thing to have a one night stand with some PK "chick" (as Crichton is so fond of calling the women) instead of sleeping with the woman — Aeryn — he loves.

He justifies it by saying that Jena's motives were pure (she is there to help people and keep the planet out of the hands of the evil Scarrans), she took care of him (by threatening to kill him a knifepoint, I guess), she's good looking and Aeryn has been mean to him. It seems that he was the one who blew her off at their final meeting, but revisionist history is so much more convenient to manipulating a storyline. Last time I checked, most guys don't behave this way. And Crichton really hasn't been portrayed as this kind of guy before. The Crichton/Jena sex scene just screams RATINGS PLOY. I mean, how else can you justify this kind of bull droppings? And how convenient for her to have a fully furnished campsite so close by that is still completely secret.

How exactly does the Sebacean pregnancy cycle work? If you look at the timeline, Crichton has only been on this planet for a few days. If they took a DNA sample early on, Katralla would have had to have been fertile at that moment in order for the impregnation to work. And then, if Sebacean physiology is anything like human physiology, you have to wait at least two weeks before you can confirm conception. If that was the timeline, it was not at all clear. Will the child also be in suspended animation for eighty cycles? (My wife found the idea of being pregnant for eighty cycles the most horrific aspect of this episode.) Or is the child "grown" in some kind of tank outside of her body?

By the end of the episode, D'Argo and Crichton both have children they have lost. Though D'Argo's chances of seeing Jothee again are reasonable, Crichton will be long dead before his daughter is even born.

In terms of the D'Argo/Chiana relationship, it turns out they are not genetically compatible. Although they brush it off initially, the idea lingers. How will this knowledge affect their relationship? Does D'Argo want to have a family? And if so, is Chiana the woman with whom he'd raise children? She seems too independent, too distrustful at this point to commit to anything long term. It puts a spin on the relationship that will be touched on again in upcoming episodes.

Moving on to the Aeryn subplot, there are pros and cons here too. For those of you who didn't get it the first fifteen times, Kemper has Dregon articulate why Aeryn can't fall in love.

And what about that fall? Wanting to give Kemper the benefit of the doubt, I checked with a number of my friends who are avid rock climbers. In a nutshell, here's what works and doesn't work about this sequence. Aeryn says she's just anchored both of them at a position above her. Even if Dregon had caused Aeryn to lose her footing as depicted, both of them falling is not the obvious outcome. The anchor above Aeryn's head is there to prevent just this type of accident from occurring. It's possible for both climbers to be hanging on the rope and struggling to regain their footing. It is possible that Dregon was not anchored between himself and Aeryn. It's possible that Aeryn's anchor was improperly secured. But seasoned climbers don't just fall like that. My climbing friends agreed, after watching the sequence, that the reason the rope broke (we see the frayed end in a later shot) was probably left on the cutting room floor.

Aeryn's leg break must not have been too bad for her to have been able to walk on it, but could she have withstood the pain for so long and dragged Dregon along without passing out from exhaustion? And what was wrong with Dregon anyway that he couldn't walk, but he's okay enough to tell Aeryn just exactly what's wrong with her love life? This whole sequence felt like a giant set-up for that mushy conversation. Oh the joy of love. Oh the pain. Oh get over it!

Aeryn's upbringing and her admission in "The Way We Weren't" make it clear that for her, as for many other PeaceKeepers, there's a difference between sex and love. What might have been more interesting would have been to create a scenario which mirrors Crichton's liaison with Jena. Let Aeryn and Drago climb to the top of their mountain and make camp. Let them get cozy by firelight. And then let them have their conversation. Let us see Aeryn make a choice in the moment the way Crichton does. Will she sleep with Dregon just because he's an attractive male and she's an adult woman with adult desires? Will she have sex with Dregon and call John's name (a cliche, I know, but Kemper seems to revel in them anyway), will she choose not to be intimate with Dregon but gain some insight into her own motives and feelings? As it stands, the Aeryn storyline is throwaway. What do we learn about her? Nothing we don't already know.

What ends up working in this story arc is probably not at all what Kemper intended — the bits and pieces of information we get that fill in the holes. In this case, it's Scorpius' backstory. How interesting that he's a Scarran/ Sebacean offspring. This would account for his telepathic abilities, but his humanoid appearance. Seeing the cooling rods in his brain in an earlier episode certainly raised the question of what kind of creature he was, and now we know. I loved the dichotomy of craving what will kill you. How ironic that Sebeceans are intolerant of heat and Scarrans desire it. How fascinating the way he has dealt with it.

The Scarran emissary says Scorpius is a mistake. Does that mean he was part of an experimental breeding program? The result of a love affair between a Scarran and Sebacean (which seems even more unlikely than a Luxan/

Sebacean one)? The result of rape? An episode focusing on Scorpius would be fantastic as he's become one of the most interesting break-out characters in the show.

Given his ability to drag his fingers through the acid pool and his quick recovery from the heat prostration after the Scarran is killed, it seems pretty clear he was faking his earlier weakness. But for what purpose? Why risk Crichton being injured or killed when Crichton holds the key to what Scorpius wants.

The other character who fares quite well in this arc is Zhaan. Ms. Hey does a wonderful job of bringing Zhaan's sense of righteous indignation to the fore. Her scenes with Pilot are fully realized. Note that the DRD who helps her suck Keheynu into the engine is the same one Crichton repaired in the first episode. And let us not forget the possibilities this sequence set up. If this was a test to see how Zhaan will defend and protect Moya, what is to come?

Overall, this story arc was unsuccessful. It certainly has its moments, though, and all of the characters are allowed at least one scene in which their talents shine. The lighting, set, music and costumes are superb throughout. I was very impressed with the way the set created a sense of place, the costumes a sense of a foreign yet familiar culture — in this case the princess was not born to the purple, but to the red. Red and white, in some pagan cultures, represent the light and those who fight the forces of darkness. In the Italian strega mythology, those who wear red and white are guardians — protectors and warriors who serve the greater good. The cleaness of white, the sense of purity is nicely balanced against the red, a sense of blood, family, obligation and continuity of the race through controlled procreation and an unwavering sense of justice.

The use of lighting, especially in the scene directly following John's space walk, was incredible. Using light to isolate, to unite and connect really augmented the overall feeling of the episode. The lighting and and the use of fades in the sequence in which D'Argo and Chiana say farewell to Crichton after he's been turned into a statue are really memorable.

And as always, the unsung heroes of any episode are the sound and music folks. For a sense of how barren the episode would be without sound effects or music, pay particular attention to the lack of music and augmented sound in the teasers that often run during the show prior to Farscape.

Perhaps Kemper should stick to producing and let the writers he's hired do the actual composing. No one questions that he and Rockne O'Bannon share a vision of this incredible universe that's compelling, but at this point, Kemper isn't a good enough writer to be responsible for such an important aspect of the show, at least not alone. A decent writing mentor and editor would be a good first step.

Grade: D
Grade for "Look at the Princess:" C-

Episode 10213: Beware of Dog
Location: Aboard Moya. Close by a Commerce Planet
Guest Cast:
Wayne Pygram as Scorpius
Writer: Naren Shankar
Director: Tony Tilse

SYNOPSIS:

Chiana and D'Argo, hoping to solve the possible parasite problem with the newly purchased store of food, barter for a Vorc and bring him aboard Moya. The creature's sole purpose in life is to sniff out a particular parasite and eradicate it. The problem is that neither Chiana nor D'Argo could fully understand the finer points of the Vorc's physiology due to a language barrier the translator microbes couldn't fully compensate for and the result is a series of mishaps which result, ultimately, in the poor creature's death.

The parasites manage to infect Rygel early on in the story and literally assume his shape, encasing the "real" Rygel inside a nasty cocoon reminiscent of the one which cocooned loggers in The X-Files epsode "Darkness Falls." When D'Argo is wounded during a confrontation by what the crew assumes is the parasite, he's infected by parasite Rygel. This little piece of information is easy to miss if you're not paying attention as all Rygel does is touch his slimy toady fingers to D'Argo's mouth (eeeww!) and the parasite enters. Not quite as nasty as the usual through the ear entryway (a.l.a. Animorphs or the Star Trek parasites), but effective nevertheless. D'Argo becomes deathly ill within moments and while Zhaan works on some sort of anti-toxin, the others attempt to track down the Vorc and the parasite.

This proves more difficult than they first imagined resulting in a series of hilarious encounters including Aeryn shoving the unfortunate creature off her bed three times for using it as his toilet and then having to put up with having her leather-clad leg humped while D'Argo tells her to just let the Vorc do its business. The sight gag here is priceless.

Eventually, the crew figures out that the Vorc has two forms: The tracker form and the warrior form. The tracker form is the harmless looking, almost huggable E.T.-clone while the warrior form comes equipped with nasty scimitar appendages which are particularly useful for slicing open the cocoons the parasite uses. By the time they manage to figure this out however, the Vorc has been mortally wounded. In the end, D'Argo is healed, Rygel is freed and we are treated to a bizarre tableau of Aeryn holding the dying Vorc while John looks on like the creature's surrogate father.

Throughout the episode, Crichton seems to be on

the verge of a nervous breakdown. He's playing chess with himself, talking out loud with no one else in the room and possibly even hallucinating. We come to learn, however, that the hallucinations he's having are only partially in his head. He's the one who actually first spots the Vorc in its warrior form, but no one believes him as he's seemed a bit off anyway. His visions of Scorpius, compounded with the fact that Scorpius might have actually damaged Crichton's brain or embedded something to bring him toward the brink of madness, are horrific. He is, as we have seen, truly terrified of the Aurora Chair and will do pretty much anything to avoid it.

CRITIQUE:

Like the recycled creatures from Dark Crystal that Zhaan encountered in "Out of their Minds," Henson again makes use of a familiar face — so to speak — in this episode: E.T. This E.T., however, is a sexually mature member of its race, as witnessed by his ... fondness for Aeryn's leather boots. There's a lot to like about this episode, and after the seriousness of the "Look at the Princess" story arc, we were all ready for a little comic relief.

What really works here is the comedic timing and the sight gags. The cast (aside from Zhaan who spends all her time at a lab table trying to find a cure for D'Argo) gets a chance to play at least one scene for laughs. The camaraderie the characters have come to feel for each other during this extended journey is revealed in these small moments. It's clear that the actors have clearly clicked as a team and the terrific chemistry is visible.

Additionally, the music for this episode is really outstanding. Pay attention to the use of bassoon and harpsichord passages to give a lighthearted flavor to the funniest scenes and how the introduction of clarinet, tympani and strings changes the mood in just a moment.

Many people don't realize how much music completes an episode by evoking mood and creating atmosphere but it's actually one of the most crucial elements of making a show work. And although Gus Gross has done fine work throughout the series, this episode is remarkable.

The characters' interpersonal relationships continue to be expanded as well. While John and Aeryn are beginning to come off as the old married couple (comfortable with each other but interspersed with moments of passion), D'Argo and Chiana occupy the position of "the lovers." They're allowed to explore the emotional and sexual landscape of an adult relationship while Aeryn and John are limited primarily to a relationship with its roots in physical desire that is blocked by Aeryn's distrust of love (as opposed to sex) and the isolation of her upbringing. The image of Aeryn cradling the Vorc as he dies his touching death, understood at last and appreciated for his noble sacrifice as John stands behind Aeryn like a protective and slightly emotionally bewildered Papa merely drives this point home with a sledge hammer.

Realizing as they do late in the game that the Vorc actually does not have the ability to communicate through language explains why the translator microbes didn't work. Set up as John and Aeryn's "child," the fact that the Vorc can be understood but cannot communicate is an interesting link to current studies which show that an infant's ability to understand spoken language is far greater than his or her ability to express it.

Zhaan, unfortunately, is starting to sound like a broken bitch record. She tells Chiana to shut up and get the hell out of the lab so she can work on a cure for D'Argo. This lack of compassion is disturbing and not adequately defined. Is she just in a bad mood or is this a continuation of the internal struggle between murderer and priestess? Can she not understand or appreciate that Chiana's lover may not survive the day? It seemed pointless for her to go after Chiana like that and leaves a bitter taste behind.

Do my eyes deceive me or does D'Argo seem to be pulling away from Chiana? Since they both know they're not genetically compatible, and therefore cannot create a child, will their relationship end?

Although the character creation of the Vorc here is extraordinary, especially the warrior form which was scary and exotic at once -- a wholly believable entity, there are some really glaring continuity and plot holes. The biggest one has to do with the Vorc. The tracker self is seen spitting the warrior part out of his mouth. But there aren't two Vorc's, only one. Crichton tries to rationalize this as some kind of shape shifting, but the presentation is confusing and contradictory. Either the Vorc is a shape shifter or it isn't. Is it a symbiotic relationship like the one between symbiot and Trill host in the Star Trek universe? There's no reason not to show it shape shifting if that's how it manifests its two forms. If that's not the case, at least we should see the warrior form re-entering the tracker form. That's just sloppy work on the part of the creative team.

Second, if the DRDs have access to every part of the ship, why are there no access doors into Command? If there are — and there does seem to be one in the bottom of the door — why didn't Crichton and the others simply roll the smoke bombs in through the DRD access door? If you argue it's for dramatic effect, you'd be right. But it's not logical.

Third, how exactly is D'Argo cured? He's suddenly all better and the explanation offered is not at all satisfactory. Did this segment end up on the cutting room floor?

I am so tired of Crichton constantly calling the female crew members "girls." Though he's supposed to be your basic All American Male, he has proven time and again that he has sensitive, intuitive aspects as well as the machismo to be a rocket jockey. Why this constant sexist comment? It's such an old and tired cliché. Just once, I'd like Aeryn to say, "I'm a woman, John, or have you forgotten?"

Aside from the plot problems, this was a very enjoyable episode, a much needed bit of comedy in what will soon become a very dark story arc.

Grade: B

Episode 10214: Won't Get Fooled Again
Location: The Earth in John's Mind, Commerce Planet
Guest Cast:
Wayne Pygram as Scorpius
Lani Tupu as Captain Bailar Crais
Kent McCord as Jack Crichton
Murray Bartlett as DK
Carmen Duncan as Leslie Crichton
Thomas Hargrove as Grath
Writer: Richard Manning
Director: Rowan Woods

SYNOPSIS:

A familiar shot opens this episode: The launch of the Farscape 1. John Crichton is piloting the module and everything looks great. Then, suddenly a huge electromagnetic wave seems to come from out of nowhere. When it collides with Farscape 1, the small craft is buffeted about and then sucked into the nexus of the wave, which, as it turns out, is a wormhole that dumps IASA astronaut John Crichton into another universe.

This familiar sequence is followed by Crichton waking up in a very Earth-like medical exam room. Jack Crichton, back turned, is talking to someone on a cell phone. As John wakes, his father turns. He's been out for a week — but strangely is in a room with no equipment. Crichton, suspecting that this is another of the Ancients' scenarios ("A Human Reaction"), embraces his father and then hurls them both off the table onto the floor. While this answers the boxers or briefs question, it also brings several buff orderlies running — and one Dr. Bettina Fairchild who bears a striking resemblance to Aeryn Sun. Crichton calls her name, but she doesn't know him. Moments later he's been sedated.

When Crichton wakes up a bit later, he's in another room in restraints. Dr. Fairchild is there again, peeking into his ears and down his throat. She tells him he's running a bit of a fever. Crichton tries again to make contact with the person he thinks is Aeryn, hoping that she'll give him some sort of sign that she's aware of their predicament. When that's unsuccessful, he finally passes his strange behavior off on the fact that the doctor reminds him of an old girlfriend.

She releases him and Crichton, thinking of the men's loo trick he used to break out of the Ancients' reality in "A Human Reaction," makes a bee-line for the nearest washroom. This time, it's the women's, and the patron inside is unamused. Next, Crichton grabs a newspaper from a passing man, but the news seems current. So far, all of Crichton's tricks aren't working.

In the lounge area of the hospital, John apologizes to his father, who responds that he, too, had a rough time after John's mother died. To Crichton, this seems like a nonsequitur, but before he can pursue it, DK arrives.

DK immediately begins complaining about how he's tired of taking all the heat for the failed mission. He goes on to tell John that the money men are looking for a scapegoat and it looks like John, because he was the craft's pilot, is the most likely candidate. Jack's angry retort about the failure residing with the weather forecasters takes the conversation into petty bickering. Jack ends by saying that Dr. Fairchild won't formally release John from her medical care until he sees a psychiatrist.

Dr. Jane Kaminski's office is a traditional book-lined

affair with a beautiful wood desk and the proverbial couch. Crichton, still looking for a loophole uses the doctor's phone to order a pizza, but before he can finish, Dr. Kaminski enters the room.

It's Zhaan, looking stunning but professionally reserved in a three-piece suit. When he mentions that he has a problem with his psychiatrist being not only a plant, but also blue, she confronts his "racism" by asking him if he has a problem with "people of color." Plants of color would be more like it. Again, Crichton tries to see whether or not Zhaan is in on the scheme, but she's not the Zhaan he knows. They haven't shared Unity and she clearly has none of her special priestess powers. Crichton is disappointed, but not surprised.

After the appointment, Crichton is walking with DK in an above ground parking lot when they're practically run down by the newest fly-boy in town: Gary Raygell (this is a phonetic approximation of the spelling of this name), who looks a lot like D'Argo in golf pants and driving gloves. DK says that D'Argo's tentacles have to do with his choice of lifestyle. It's clear that DK hates Raygel, but once Raygel mentions the word beer, Crichton ditches the whiny DK in a flash.

At a local bar, D'Argo and Crichton proceed to become extremely drunk and D'Argo indulges Crichton's ramblings about how he's not going to play this time and how he's got it all figured out. As he's twirling around in his chair, he takes in the band for the first time. There, working his mojo on drums, is Scorpius. And Pilot is grooving out nearby as the resident bongo player.

But Crichton's attention is diverted by the arrival of Dr. Fairchild who greets Crichton warmly, but then climbs onto D'Argo's lap and begins flirting with him. This doesn't please Crichton too much. He goes to the bar to get another pitcher of beer and Scorpius slides onto the stool next to his. Crichton thinks he's either seeing doubles or twins, but Scorpius tells him it's neither and that Scorpius is actually the only one in the whole scenario who is real. Then suddenly, he departs, leaving Crichton with more questions.

Back in Dr. Kaminski's office, Crichton spends his time trying to figure out Scorpius' motivations. It then occurs to Crichton that he might have completely snapped and is lying in a twitching heap on Moya while his crewmates stand around and watch. Another possibility is that he's still on Moya but is hallucinating. When Zhaan agrees that's possible, it doesn't seem to make John feel any better.

At the base, Jack Crichton tells his son that there's a new administrator on board who wants to meet Crichton. When it turns out to be Rygel, Crichton's behavior becomes, to his father and the others, acutely bizarre. He systematically flips Rygel's (a.k.a. D. Logan) business cards into Rygel's face, steals his cigar and smokes it and plays with a model of the Farscape 1 as though it were a toy. At first, it seems that Crichton has almost convinced himself that he's gone crazy, but when Rygel begins talking about trying the Farscape project again, Crichton gets a sudden feeling that there is actually someone else behind this facade, someone who wants the wormhole technology the Ancients placed in Crichton's brain.

But Crichton isn't buying it and when confronted by Rygel in the parking lot a few minutes later, he grabs Rygel out of the golf cart he's been riding in and flings him over the edge of the circular stairwell. Rygel falls some four or five storeys to his supposed death. Needless to say DK and Jack are appalled at John's behavior. Crichton tells DK he's nothing more than a mindless wimp who's afraid he'll lose his job if the project fails. He tells Jack Crichton that his father is just angry that John won't behave in the way Jack expects him to. Then he pushes past them and returns to the bar.

In a secluded booth in the back, John finds Chiana nuzzling Aeryn's neck. As he slides into the booth, Crichton is introduced to "Jessica" and when Aeryn turns her attention once again to D'Argo, Chiana/Jessica tells Crichton she has a thing for astronauts. To Crichton, this is the best news he's heard all day. But his perfect moment is spoiled by Scorpius hissing at him from the adjoining booth. Crichton tells him to go away and suggests to the others that they go for a drive.

In D'Argo's fancy red convertible, Crichton speeds down an almost deserted highway. Scorpius appears on the windshield. Clearly, he's trying to talk to John, but Crichton isn't interested. In one of the show's truly hilarious moments, Crichton tries to get Scorpius off by using the windshield wipers. It seems pretty clear that Crichton doesn't see any way out of this world, which is becoming crazier and stranger at every turn. Finally, he steers the car into the path of an oncoming truck. Everyone screams...

...and John wakes up in a hospital exam room. Dr. Fairchild comes in, wearing a set of huge blue plastic curlers, her only injury, it seems, from the head-on collision. She tells him that everybody's fine and that he has a visitor. He thinks it'll be dear old Dad, but it's not. It's Leslie Crichton, John's mother. She's been dead for five years. When Leslie bemoans the man John's become and all he's lost in the process, Crichton counters that he had to change in order to survive. She touches his head, tells him he's sweating. She embraces him. Crichton looks close to tears, but before she can undo him completely, he flees.

Back in the bar, Crichton takes a seat next to Scorpius and tells the Scarran/Sebacean hybrid that he's ready to listen now. But it's the wrong guy. This Scorpius doesn't know Crichton. Suddenly Leslie appears again, only this time, she's in a hospital gown and pushing an IV pole. She begs John to stay with her. She pleads with him not to abandon her on her deathbed. Crichton runs again.

At the base, Crichton is harassed by a beat cop — Bailar Crais. When Crais tries to arrest him, Crichton takes

Crais' pistol and nearly beats the other man to death with is fists.

Next Crichton finds himself in D. Logan's office, with Rygel/Logan alive and well. DK is there, along with Jack, Dr. Fairchild/Aeryn and Dr. Kaminski/Zhaan. The walls are lined with incongruous photos, including one of Scorpius proudly holding a gold record, probably for his rendition of "I've Got You Under My Skin" or perhaps "Someone to Watch Over Me." Crichton is sweating profusely now. He shoots Jack, but the bullet passes right through him and shatters one of the pictures on the wall. He fires again, screaming for them to stop. The assembled crew becomes disinterested in Crichton and starts discussing what they want for lunch.

Back in the medical exam room, handcuffed to a chair, Crichton is presented a ticket for numerous offenses by Bailar Crais, who is holding a dog he calls Toto. After Crais leaves, Scorpius appears and tells Crichton that he's being held prisoner by a Scarran. Crichton, frightened enough to really listen now, tries to take in all that Scorpius is telling him about how to kill the Scarran and why he's been sweating since he supposedly arrived on "Earth." The Scarran, Scorpius says, is going to try and break Crichton using induced hallucinations and that Scorpius is there to protect him. During Crichton's time with Scorpius on that Gammak Base, Scorpius imbedded a chip in John's brain which has now activated as a kind of fail-safe against the Scarran's attempt to worm his way into Crichton's brain. If Crichton can focus on what are his real memories and separate them from the reality the Scarran is creating, he might very well survive. Scorpius senses the Scarran is preparing for another interrogation session and flees to avoid detection. And, not surprisingly, Crichton has found himself between a rock and a hard place.

Crichton begins to sweat again as the Scarran comes closer, in response to the heat the Scarran gives off. The hallucinations are shorter in duration now, and becoming stranger and stranger. First, Crichton finds himself strapped to a exam table with Zhaan (dressed in a fetching leather outfit), Chiana (looking definitely not-innocent in a school-girl uniform) and Aeryn in a nurse's outfit reminiscent of the one on the cover of Blink 182's first album, bending over his ... well the sexual innuendo is explicit enough here, complete with a rather graphic demonstration with an old-style syringe. This sequence is shot down Crichton's body. Fortunately for the ratings board, he's clothed.

Then Rygel appears, replete in dominatrix leather mask and begins whipping Crichton with a mean (or enticing, depending on your point of view) cat-o-nine-tails.

From there, we jump to the "Mommy Ward" where Crichton is surrounded by screaming babies and then by his screaming parents who are arguing about whether or not he's better than a terrier. He's dumped off the roof, landing right in front of Bailar Crais' cop car. Crais, wearing a very smart pair of red pumps, shouts a strange and unintelligible version of the Miranda warning, but when Crichton tells him that he doesn't understand, Crais retorts that if Crichton doesn't understand then Crais can't arrest him. He speeds off.

And Crichton finds himself sitting in D'Argo/Gary's convertible overlooking a lovely cityscape. D'Argo, doing an impression of an overly effeminate drag queen confesses that he's been having special thoughts about Crichton for some time. He wants Crichton to participate in a special Luxan ritual involving his qualta blade, some questionable lubricant and ... Chiana, who wants to watch. From there, poor Crichton finds himself back in Zhaan's office. His mother, wearing a teddy and a silk robe open down the front, pulls a book about Freud's Oedipus Complex from the shelf and asks John if she can explain it to him. He's confused. He's repulsed. He's ... almost kissing his mother. And he's bounced back to the bar, which has become a disco, complete with mirror ball. While Aeryn and Chiana get down on the dance floor, D'Argo does a decent Saturday Night Fever imitation.

Suddenly Aeryn Sun is there screaming for everyone to get off the dance floor. She tells John that she found him beneath the surface of the Commerce Planet and has come to rescue him. She says she's killed Scorpius. When she won't let him leave, Crichton's suspicion that she's not his princess in shining armor is confirmed. She leaves him. Crichton finds himself in the disco again and shortly thereafter goes into convulsions.

Finally, we see Crichton's torture chamber. He is indeed the prisoner of a Scarran who keeps turning up the heat, so to speak, in an effort to extract whatever he's after. But he goes too far and ends up killing Crichton. Crichton collapses onto the floor. Moments later, his hand twitches on his pulse pistol. It begins to emit a high-pitched whine. The Scarran comes closer to investigate and Crichton shoves the pistol into the Scarran's mouth. It overloads and blows his head off.

Scorpius appears. He commends John for breaking free, even though Scorpius did help by stopping his brain functions for a moment or so to give the illusion of death. When Crichton says he's going to find a way to get the chip out of his head, Scorpius seems surprised. He doesn't know anything about a chip. As Crichton starts to argue, his words become jumbled and his seems to lose his thought. Scorpius smiles and tells John that how to return to the surface, reassuring Crichton their time together is far from over.

CRITIQUE:

In keeping with the frequent pop culture references that inform Crichton's speech and consciousness, "Won't Get Fooled Again" is a complex homage not only to contemporary culture, but also to the basic nature of human thought and emotion.

Beginning with the episode's title, which is also the title of a classic song by Pete Townsend (for a great acoustic version of it, check out The Secret Policeman's Other Ball). In terms of the episode it's an obvious reference to "A Human Reaction," a classic episode from Season 1 in which Crichton thinks he's returned to Earth only to learn that he's been part of a vast experiment by the Ancients. When he wakes up in a hospital that looks like Earth, he's determined not to be fooled again. It turns out that he is — and isn't — fooled. That there's something going on with inside his head. And that Scorpius is somehow involved. Additionally, the song's lyrics refer to the new boss (substitute any power grubbing institution here) being exactly the same as the old boss. A nice double entrendre here. Rygel, is the "new boss" in charge of Crichton's project and he's just as money-conscious and power hungry as the old project director had been. Aboard Moya, Rygel is often the personification of the worst of what an individual can be: Self-absorbed, self-centered, power-hungry and money-hungry. It's no accident that Crichton's subconscious puts Rygel in this position.

And speaking of Crichton's subconscious, what a rich field for mining here! Every one of the main players in Crichton's life in the Uncharted Territories play important roles. And writer Manning has done a nice job of fitting them neatly into their respective places, thus revealing Crichton's true fears and providing insight into how he's making sense of this world.

Zhaan, for example, appears as a psychiatrist. Her calm answer-a-question-with-a-question method both frustrates John and gives him the space to try and sort things out. As she does aboard Moya, Zhaan functions as an emotional touchstone for John, someone who will help him see the truth of a situation. This relationship was set up nicely in Season 1's "Back and Back and Back to the

Future" but hasn't really been given the time it deserves and needs to develop further. The possibilities for Zhaan to play a more primary role in Crichton's life are really limitless — if he can conquer his libido and have a friendship with a woman who's his equal.

D'Argo appears here as friend and competitor. While he can be a great drinking buddy, he also "steals" Bettina Fairchild away from Crichton in the bar and then later propositions Crichton. Longing for male companionship, Crichton looks for that in D'Argo, but the truth is that D'Argo is emotionally too young for an adult friendship. Mr. Simcoe, talking about how he approaches playing D'Argo has said he sees the character as more of an adolescent, even though he's thirty cycles old. The fact that D'Argo is impulsive, hot-headed and (in later episodes) more interested in doing the horizontal mambo with Chiana than anything else helps bring out these younger male qualitites. Interesting enough, however, D'Argo has never expressed an interest in Aeryn and John has openly refused Chiana's overtures on more than one occasion. Yet Crichton still sees D'Argo as competition in the deeper parts of his mind.

Aeryn translates into the symbol of the unattainable woman. She won't engage with him in the treatment room when he first wakes up and has absolutely no recollection of him. This is one of Crichton's first clues that this time it's different. In "A Human Reaction," Aeryn was, at the very least, his ally. She maintains her unavailable status throughout much of the episode: Kissing D'Argo in the bar, nuzzling with Chiana and then later dancing with her. Near the end, however, her image is used to try and pursuade Crichton. By this time, however, he's too distrustful. As a mirror of Crichton's waking confusion and frustration with Aeryn's go away/come here approach to their relationship, the sub-conscious is right on the mark.

Chiana doesn't really get much leeway here. She's seen as loose aboard Moya and that's exactly how she's portrayed in John's mind as well. She's the good-time girl, the party girl, the one who finds astronauts a turn-on. In the well of John's subconscious, Chiana and Aeryn are interchangable. She becomes the fourth member of a weird double-dating scenario.

The fact that he envisions Chiana and Aeryn together is also no surprise, given his gender and sexual orientation. One has to wonder, though, whether this scene and the one in which John is being poked, prodded and restrained by three leather-clad females was motivated by the titilation factor more than anything else. Personally, at times I felt as though I had more information about Crichton than I really wanted.

Pilot plays a very minor role here, as he does in Crichton's life aboard Moya. Crichton's not connected to Pilot and Moya the way Aeryn is, or Zhaan. In some ways, it seems as though he hasn't quite figured out what to make of the symbiotic relationship they have.

Reducing Crais to a beat cop who is a bit odd from the outset and then becomes downright weird and annoying also seems appropriate. Crichton allows himself to unleash the physical violence he's held in check and all Crais can do is issue him a citation. My personal favorite scene was Crais in red pumps. Now that's not something that you see everyday.

In terms of Crichton's Earth-bound friends and family, there's some new ground covered here as well. Crichton's deeper feelings about DK suggest that DK was more passive and overly concerned with what other people will think of him. His association with Crichton brings him prestige, but that's only good as long as Crichton is currently in favor with the powers that be. As soon as Crichton stops playing by the unspoken rules, DK worries primarily about how he will be affected rather than about John's mental health.

Jack Crichton, the all-powerful father figure, doesn't gain much depth here. We know that John has mixed feelings about his father. He loves and respects him. He wants to please Jack. He wants to be like his father yet at the same time resents the fact that he's known as his father's son. This is a classic father-son conflict pattern and like any man Crichton's age, he hasn't quite worked it all through.

But it's Crichton's mother, Leslie, who is deeply intwined in so many facets of John's personality. In this episode we witness his guilt over leaving her deathbed as well as his inner conflict regarding what he's had to lose in order to become successful. Mothers, especially of little boys, are probably the only ones who truly know their sons. They see them at their most vulnerable, their most precious and then they see what the world does to them. Leslie, too, had to contend with Jack's expectations of their son and it's clear that there was another side to him that he's all but buried as he grew into adulthood.

The sequence involving Freud's Oedipus theory explained is the only piece of this that I didn't find particularly interesting. The Oedipus story, originally writtten as a Greek Tragedy that was part of a larger cycle of tragic plays, tells the story of a couple who are told by an oracle that their son will kill his father and marry his mother. Trying to avoid this outcome, the son is taken into the hills and abandoned. But a kindly shepherd finds him and raises the boy as his own. When he's grown, he returns to Thebes, the town of his birth, and accidentally kills his father. He then falls in love with his mother and marries her. They have children. Eventually, because Fate cannot be outwitted, the truth is revealed. The mother kills himself and Oedipus pokes out his own eyes.

Freud, who many call the founder of modern psychoanalysis, but who was probably one of the greatest mysognists who ever lived, proposed that all boys secretly want to kill their fathers so they can have their mothers for their own. This became known as the Oedipus Complex. For Crichton to harbor sexual feelings for his mother is to be expected. Sexual development has many stages and aspects. Because a mother figure is so powerful and present in a child's life and because all children desire to be the center of attention, it makes perfect sense that a child would want to eliminate any competitor for their mother's love and attention. The father figure is the major competitor. When a child becomes aware of his or her own sexuality and realizes that their parents are sexual beings, this information is stored and process according to the cultural norms.

In many cultures, sexual contact between parents and adolescents is prohibited. But in some cultures, the parents are responsible for the sexual initiation of their children. For those of us raised in Western cultures, this idea is off-putting if not downright disgusting. This, however, is not genetic, it's cultural. And because it's not genetic, it's normal for Crichton to have these feelings, but because he was raised in an American contemporary culture, he has been taught that these feelings are wrong. The basic problem I found in introducing this aspect into the episode was that it was predictable, and so much of this episode was strange and weird and full of the unexpected that it just felt like filler.

Overall, however, this is a fine episode. Although it doesn't work as a stand-alone story because there are so many references to what's gone before, it's a fine piece of writing and holds up to multiple viewings.

Grade: A

Episode 10215: The Locket
Location: Time-Altering Mist Above a Dead World
Guest Cast:
Wayne Pygram as Scorpius
Paul Goddard as Stark
Allyson Standen as Ennixx

Writer: Justin Monjo
Director: Ian Watson

SYNOPSIS:

Crichton is waiting for Aeryn. She's been gone twenty-four arns. Communication was lost some time before. John is joined in Command by D'Argo and the others, including Stark who has come to return the borrowed transport pod and bring some important news. When the crew finally has word of Aeryn, they're overjoyed to hear her voice again. She arrives greatly altered, however. She's aged one-hundred-sixty cycles in the space of one solar day. Crichton and the others are stunned — at the state of decay of the transport pod, not to mention the "decay" of Aeryn herself. Opinions are offered. Zhaan confirms that this is really Aeryn. Aeryn thrashes and cries and tells them she must get back to the planet or her granddaughter will die.

Chiana and Rygel, in typical fashion, board the transport pod looking for treasures. D'Argo chastises Chiana, claiming her actions demean her. He tells her to go and sit with Aeryn. She resists. He shouts. She curses and walks away.

Thinking her delirious, deranged or worse, Aeryn has been made to rest. She wakes to find Chiana at her bedside, but manages to distract Chiana long enough to drug her with a knock-out hypospray and escapes in the now-ancient transport pod. Crichton, unwilling to let her go, takes a second pod after her. Planetside, angered at Crichton's bull-headedness, she tells him that if he wants a full explanation, he should return in eight arns. But when he tries to go back, the opening between Moya and the planet vanishes and he's forced to return to the inhospitable world.   On board Moya, Zhaan retreats into meditation. Stark seeks her out and tells her about an ancient theory that says there are places in the space-time continuum, called Center Halos, in which all the possible dimensions exist simultaneously. Although time outside the halo continues, time inside slows and eventually, as the halo hardens, ceases to exist altogether. He tells Zhaan that he's heard Delvians are able to sense the slipstream of time and proposes they share Unity to test his idea. Zhaan agrees, although she fears that his mind may overpower hers.

Their sharing is indeed powerful, causing ripples throughout the ship. After meeting with the others, the crew come to the realization that as soon as the mist around them hardens completely, they will be trapped in time — or out of it — forever.

When Chiana wakes, D'Argo takes her aside and tells her that, essentially, she doesn't have to steal any more since she is one of the crew. She reminds him that not only does she do what she wants, but he also cannot change her. He agrees, albeit almost ruefully. Chiana, looking at him and seeing him with both the eyes of love and the clarity of experience, notes that their approaches to living are very different. While D'Argo's life has been circumscribed by the Luxan code of honorable behavior, a warrior's training and many painful experiences and losses, Chiana has used whatever means she has at her disposal at any one time to survive. She wonders whether their relationship will survive given their differences.

Meanwhile, years have passed on the world below. Crichton, restless and bored, still talks with the visions of Scorpius in his head and is often the topic of conversation between Aeryn and her granddaughter. After fifty-five cycles pass, Aeryn, Crichton and Ennixx once again make the journey to the barren world in the hopes of seeing the "gate" into the mist open. Aeryn tells Ennixx that she needs to die in space and they part, leaving a transport pod so that Ennixx can return to her life on one of the other planets in the system. After several tries, Crichton's com signal reaches Moya. He's overjoyed to be going home, despite the passage of time.

On the short journey back, however, Aeryn dies of old age (at more than two hundred cycles) and the crew finds Crichton bent over her still form. Crichton, now about eight-five years old, cautions the crew about choosing life in this system. Stark in particular believes that it might be possible to escape if they could travel back the way they have come, essentially back through time. Although Pilot argues for moving forward, the others decide that it would be best to try and starburst backward because Moya is still actually in touch with the outside edge of the mist at her stern. As they starburst backward, time slows in geometric proportion to their velocity and eventually, the crew is unable to move at all. Just before this happens, Zhaan and Stark once again share Unity. Their combined powers not only allow Zhaan to contact Crichton (since they've also shared Unity, they have a special psychic bond) but also to allow Crichton to move through a kind of time corridor and manually finish the starburst procedure from Command.

Moments later, Zhaan awakes from a sudden trance, realizes they've been successful and races to Command to prevent Aeryn from initially entering the mist. She and Stark are the only ones who retain full memories of what has happened because they were Unified at the time, although Aeryn and John both retain a feeling that something special has transpired between them.

Stark tells Zhaan that their movement back through the timeline didn't necessarily wipe out Aeryn's family line as all possibilities exist at the same time and that time splinters into countless possible futures any place a Center Halo exists. Together, they go to find D'Argo. Stark gives D'Argo an image of Jothee, telling D'Argo the boy is scheduled to be sold into slavery in a few solar days. Although Zhaan assures the Luxan they will find his son, it is unclear whether or not they will have enough time to find and rescue him before the auction.

CRITIQUE:

Definitely one of the best episodes of the season, "The Locket" manages several storylines successfully. The "A" (or primary) story centering around Aeryn and Crichton is heartfelt and extraordinarily well-acted. Monjo, it seems, has recovered his sense of humanity after the debacle which passed for storytelling in "Crackers Don't Matter." Ms. Black is amazing as a well-seasoned Aeryn. Arriving on Moya for the first time in one hundred sixty cycles, she cups Crichton's face with her hand and calls him beautiful. It's obvious she's come to terms with her love for him, with her regrets about with might have been and has mellowed like a fine, rich wine. Aeryn's age makeup is wonderful and it's so satisfying to see Aeryn contented, on some level, with how her life has gone.

After Crichton is stranded in time, he gets to experience fifty-five cycles of sharing a life with Aeryn. Their scenes together just before they return to Moya are graceful and delightful. The obvious chemistry between the actors really shines here, but again Ms. Black is particularly memorable, especially in the scene without dialogue where everything is expressed through gesture, body language and a smile that actually reaches all the way to her eyes.

Although Crichton's age makeup isn't as successful, he also manages to embody the older version of himself with believable depth. His real grief at Aeryn's passing is so dead-on that several members of my watching gang were moved to tears, especially when he opens the locket to find an image of himself, knowing Aeryn claimed it contained an image of the only person she ever truly loved.

Why however, he suddenly develops an American Southern accent is a mystery. Do all aging astronauts become "good ol' boys" when they hit their eighties? This was silly and the least believable part of his character's presentation here. It reminded me of how the Star Trek writers turned Dr. McCoy into their version of a simple old country doctor during his cameo appearance in The Next Generation. By Roddenberry's twenty-fourth century, such a figure has not existed for some five hundred years. And though McCoy was old, he wasn't that old. T   h   e progression in the D'Argo storyline is very exciting. Although I would personally be saddened by the dissolution of the D'Argo / Chiana relationship, it would not surprise me given the way the writers have been handling them since they discovered they weren't genetically compatible in "Look at the Princess." And Producer David Kemper, in an online chat from August 2000 hints that this may indeed be true. Additionally, some of you will remember that during "Beware of Dog," D'Argo asks Crichton — not Chiana — to find Jothee. The re-introduction of Jothee is pretty much a given here — look at how many times he's been mentioned in recent episodes and the way in which children figure heavily in the "Look at the Princess" story arc.

Zhaan — finally! — gets some real screen time. What a wonderful affirmation of her we find in the scenes with Stark. It was nice to see Stark respond to her from a place of emotion rather than raw desire -- to come upon her naked and not give her the expected "once over" that we've seen time and again. Her willingness to risk her sanity for the sake of the others is also a welcome change from the very bitchy stance she's been relegated to of late. And Stark — how good to have him back. He's exceptionally intriguing and seems a perfect "partner" for Zhaan. Perhaps the writers will allow him to journey with Moya's crew for a time and thus make a way for Zhaan to continue to grow and reclaim her spiritual side.

Great guest casting rounds out this episode nicely. Allyson Stenden, who plays Ennixx, has remarkably similar features to Claudia Black/Aeryn and the actors hired to portray Ennixx's children could easily be from the same gene pool.   Finally, whoever was in charge of continuity didn't do the math for this one. Aeryn says she's "lived" for 165 cycles; Zhaan says she's been gone for 160. If the "gate" opens every 55 cycles, then a 24 arn span of time would add up to 165 cycles (given that the "gate" opens every 8 arns, from Moya's perspective). What Aeryn really must mean is that she's lived for 185 cycles, otherwise, she would have been five cycles old when she left Moya.

We also find out that Crichton was born around 1965 as he says he was about four when the Apollo 11 crew landed on the moon in 1969. If the show is running in "real" time — it's now the year 2000 on Crichton's Earth, that would make him 35, a bit older than I'd guessed. Finally, Crichton says he's kept his com badge safe for 50 cycles (does that mean he kept it unprotected for the first 5 years?) and Aeryn says she's lived 200 cycles near the time of her death when it should be 210. Maybe the "more than" got left out somewhere in the revisions or on the cutting room floor.

Grade: A

Episode 10216: The Ugly Truth
Location: A Plokavian Vessel in the Uncharted Territories
Guest Cast:
Lani Tupu as Captain Bailar Crais
Paul Goddard as Stark
Peter Carroll as the Plokavian Gahv
Linda Cropper as the Plokavian Fento
Writers: Gabrielle Stanton & Harry Werksman, Jr
Director: Tony Tilse

SYNOPSIS:

"The Ugly Truth" focuses on five different versions of the same set of events. The episode's basic storyline opens with Aeryn, Crichton, D'Argo, Zaahn and Stark boarding Talyn, at Crais' request. Talyn, he tells them, is becoming too difficult to manage and is increasingly violent and unresponsive to Crais' commands. He wants to disarm Talyn by trading his main cannon for a dampening net made by the Plokavians. He needs the crew's help, especially Moya's and Aeryn's to install the net, which will require some hands-on work.

Crais, in a show of good faith, disconnects himself from Talyn and hands the neural interface to Aeryn. He claims Talyn is disarmed, but when the Plokavian's arrive at the rendezvous point, they claim Talyn has not been prepared for the net's installation. Moment's later, the Plokavian ship is destroyed by a burst from one of Talyn's energy weapons. Crais panics, reveals a second neural interface that he's secreted on his person, throws them off the ship and starbursts away.

Although the crew members make it safely to the transport pod before another Plokavian ship enters the vicinity, they are captured. Each crew member is interrogated separately about what has happened. Unfortunately, their stories don't match. The Plokavians, who claim to want only justice for their fallen comrades, see no other choice but to put all five members of the crew to death.

In the meantime, Rygel has been unable to even make contact with the Plokavian ship housing the prisoners and Pilot suggests that since they cannot influence the outcome of their shipmates' fate, their energies would be better served searching for Talyn. Rygel and Chiana reluctantly agree, but are soon frustrated and bored by the repetitive search pattern that fails to turn up any leads.

As each member of the crew is interrogated, we get a bit more information about the events and also insight into each character's perspective. Aeryn is the first to be questioned. Her story follows the one we've seen initially very closely. This first flashback sequence reinforces the fact that Aeryn is in favor of helping Crais, but both D'Argo and Crichton are vocal in their distrust of Crais' motives.

They suspect he's not telling the truth, even though he insisted his intent was pure. Aeryn claims that Talyn's defenses were on manual override — that she saw Crais put in the commands herself — and that no one was responsible for the destruction of the ship. It was a fluke. An accident.

The Plokavian interrogators draw close to Aeryn and we see that she's sitting in a chair surrounded by a pool of what may be acid. The interrogators, Gahv and Fento, seem to be dripping some kind of noxious substance from their flesh and her reaction indicates that it's either a very unpleasant smell or that she fears what the chemical will do if it comes into contact with her skin.

She is returned to a kind of giant mushroom in the middle of dense blackness. They're clearly some distance from the ground and the only way off the platform is through a caged elevator which rises from the mushroom's stem and pokes through the top. Aeryn emerges from the cage, much to everyone's relief as she was not present when they awoke after being captured. Crichton draws Aeryn close to him in an attempt to get information without being observed by the Plokavians, but is unable to share any of it with Zaahn before she is called for questioning.

Zaahn's story differs slightly. When Crais mentions the Plokavians, Zaahn leans over to Stark and tells him this race values truth and justice. It later becomes clear that she's trying to placate them by flattery and thus soften their hard-line stance about retribution. Talyn, it seems, will have to be sedated to have his main cannon traded for a dampening net, a procedure which makes Crichton and D'Argo suspicious. Crais claims he's only fired upon others in self defense and reminds them of Talyn's encounter with the Halosians ("Out of Their Minds"). When the Plokavians arrive, Zaahn draws Stark to the vid display and comments to him about how beautiful and elegant their ship is. Again, here she's trying to make points with her interrogators, but we can see how differently the stories are being told as in Aeryn's version, Zaahn and Stark did not cross the bridge, but stayed near the entrance during the entire exchange. When the Plokavians claim Crais has not adequately prepared Talyn for the procedure, the weapons array charges. Crichton moves toward the console, but Aeryn stops him before he can touch it. Talyn fires. Crais panics, throws them off the ship and starbursts away.

Stark's version of events reveals some rather ugly truths about the Plokavians. Though Stark's race is a slave race, as Crais is quick to point out, Stark is intimately familiar with the Plokavians. He calls them barbarians and murderers and is enraged that Crais would even consider trading with them. Their race makes and sells weapons and enslaves other worlds, including Stark's homeworld. Stark tells the others the Plokavians make novatine gas, which is lethal, and as we are later to discover, one of the six cargos leviathans are forbidden to carry.

Stark is returned. D'Argo, furious about being captured and helpless in his rage, attacks Stark, claiming he is responsible for their imprisonment. Clearly, not only is D'Argo angry because he runs the risk of losing his life for another's mistake, but his search for Jothee has been interrupted as well. D'Argo knocks Stark's mask off and the sudden energy surge is excruciating for Stark. He screams for help as the mask rolls dangerously toward the edge, but is retrieved moments before it slips into the darkness. He replaces it, then, visibly shaken, apologizes to the others, saying that the mask keeps his energies under control. When the mask is suddenly removed, he loses control of the energies. But if he knows he — or someone else — will take it off, then he can prepare himself in advance for the change that will occur in him.

D'Argo is the next to be interrogated. Unlike the others, he is almost eager to tell the Plokavians that Stark fired the cannon. He also tells Gahv and Fento that he was not willing to participate in Crais' plan. And while he acknowledges that he does not mourn the death of anyone who deals in novatine gas, he takes no responsibility for Stark's actions. In D'Argo's version, he and Zaahn are the ones who examine the 3D vid of the Plokavian ship and note that its cargo contains novatine gas.

While D'Argo is gone, Stark tells Zaahn that he didn't fire the cannon. She tells him that she believes him.

Crichton's "testimony" is where one of the episode's "truths" is revealed: No one will see any event the same way. Each individual is shaped by her or his perspective — literally and figuratively — and so it's only natural that the Plokavians will be getting different versions of the truth. All are true, essentially, they're just different interpretations. And he admits that because of the feelings they share, as well as the feelings they have for Moya's offspring, Talyn, some will be willing to risk and possibly sacrifice their own lives in order to save others.

The Plokavians can't grasp this. To them, all perspectives are the same, which is helpful when an culture is devoted to making weapons that enslave and massacre. It would be inconvenient to have independent thinkers who might question the wisdom of manufacturing novatine gas, among other items.

In Crichton's version, he deliberately mispronounces the Plokaviods' names, calling them Plokovians and Pleckaviods. He seems annoyed by their strategy, especially when he says something and his interrogators play back a segment of a previous session which directly conflicts with what he's said. We learn from Crichton's version that Talyn would not have willingly parted with his cannon (could the writers have made the sexual innuendo more obvious, especially coming from Crichton?) and this is why Crais needed their help to sedate the leviathan/gunship hybrid. Additionally, Crichton says that although Stark moved toward the console with the intent of firing, Crichton prevented him from doing so. Stark could not have fired the weapon, which leaves us to ponder several other possibilities.

While Crichton is gone, Stark wonders whether or not they'll be killed. And if, so, how their captors will do it. Aeryn mentions something about dispersal, which excites Stark because he believes he might be able to survive dispersal. Zaahn agrees, remembering how the sorcerer Maldis was able to reassemble himself ("Picture if You Will"). But then Stark falls into melancholy again, fearing he would not be able to transfer his energy onto another plane and survive to return at some point.

After Crichton returns, the Plokavians tell the five prisoners that since their stories don't match, they will all be killed. The Plokavians decide that Aeryn will die first. Stark, unwilling to see his friends sacrificed, confesses to destroying the Plokavian vessel. An immobilizing force field paralyzes the other crew members. Stark removes his face mask and leaves it near Zaahn. Then, he enters the caged elevator. The Plokavian interrogators tell Stark that they suspected him all along. Moments later, he's dispersed.

When the crew is reunited on Moya, we get the final bit of information about what transpired. Talyn, it seems, knew that the Plokavian ship was carrying novatine gas and Moya told him that it was one of the six forbidden cargos. It seems likely, then, that Talyn might have acted on his own.

D'Argo confesses to Chiana that he's distressed by how distrustful he is of everyone and he doesn't like the man that he's become. Crichton and Aeryn, sharing a contemplative moment in the galley wonder if Stark survived. Then Crichton asks Aeryn whether she was concerned about protecting Talyn or Crais. When she tells him her concern was solely for Talyn, Crichton is reassured that she has no feelings for Crais, a leftover question from "Mind the Baby." Zaahn, alone in her quarters, cradles Stark's mask against her and mourns.

CRITIQUE:

This episode seems like it was written by someone who's just discovered that everybody's perspective on an event will be different. This is an important revelation for an individual to experience as it allows him or her to embrace difference without feeling threatened. This aspect of the thematic message will seem obvious and even juvenile to some viewers, but some of the younger members of the audience might find it enlightening.

What any individual brings into a situation will completely shape what he or she takes away from it. Factors which influence perspective can include culture, race, gender, age and experience. Additionally, as is the case here, there is an underlying motivation to protect Talyn. And since the five crew members didn't have a chance to essentially agree on one story before being interrogated, they each contributed a bit to the shape of the tale.

Presenting a race like the Plokavians and screening this episode just before "A Clockwork Nebari" provides a nice setup for the latter episode. The Plokavians seem so overtly evil, it's easy for us to dislike them. They create weapons of mass destruction; they're physically repulsive (an obvious metaphor for the corruption within); they share a collective viewpoint which does not allow for alternative interpretations of right and wrong. As we have seen with the Nebari, difference and individuality are foreign concepts. In this way, they are like Star Trek's Borg – sharing a collective unity, a shared consciousness. This unity allows any people to put aside what may be, in the greater view, morally abhorrent acts. They claim they're searching for the truth, but when it's provided to them, they reject it because it doesn't fit into their world view. The parallels between the Plokavians, the Nebari and many human experiences are numerous. How many times have we witnessed cultures enslaved, assimilated or completely destroyed in the name of a greater good, which most of the time takes its form in religious zeal? The conquerer's unwavering belief that worshiping their god (or gods) is the only way to experience spiritual enlightenment has changed the history of our world time and again.

On one level, Crichton's statement about differing perspectives is provocative — what if we operated under the assumption that everyone is right? What if all the different names for God were actually just different forms of the same word, for example? What if, at the time of one's death, each individual experienced the afterlife in exactly the way she or he had imagined it? Eternal bliss or eternal damnation. An existential void. A rest period between lifetimes. Whatever. That the afterlife was a completely personalized experience, shaped by one's own particular version of a private or organized system of beliefs.

What's interesting about the Plokavians' reaction is that it mirrors the way humans sometimes react to a marked differences in each other — with disbelief and hostility. If you are like that, then maybe I am too! No, I'm not like that! That, in essence, is the life-altering lesson that, for some, opens up a world of possibility and for others narrows their perspectives into fear, hatred and sometimes violence.

Hopefully, as with all good storytelling, some viewers will experience some kind of personal revelation. Others might simply nod and say, "Yeah, I knew that already." But as a thematic element, it's interesting — and it's a fundamental principle of scifi: Difference makes for interesting conflicts. And conflict is an essential part of a good story, no matter what the genre.

On some level, waiting for each bit of information to be revealed was what drove the episode forward. But it's also what bogged it down. Watching the same sequence over and over became tedious, especially since some of the reactions didn't vary at all. Some judicious cutting here might have helped the pacing.

The sets of this episode were stunning, although the lights on the bendable stems reminded me of the character Bag from My Stepmother is an Alien. The makeup, was also very well done. And I loved the superimposed images of the other characters on Crichton's face during his interrogation — nice touch. But what was the set designer thinking by making the chair shaped to look like a design for a pap-smear gone bad?

I hate to see Stark go. He's really a fascinating character and his abilities are so incredible and fascinating. It was also nice to see Zhaan have a "partner" for a while, someone who is also on a spiritual quest in his own way but who seems to genuinely care for her. Her grief for him at the episode's end was heartfelt — kudos to Ms. Hey for this scene.

As for the other characters, some fare well and some don't. Chiana and Rygel are pretty much wasted here. Chiana actions are confusing. While she agrees with Pilot that their best option is to search for Talyn, she's argumentative and bored within three arns. Portraying her as that childish really didn't work. And then to have her apologize to Pilot — it was just filler. All three of those characters could have been utilized differently — speculating about Talyn's behavior or even revealing the tidbit about the novatine gas would have heightened the tension with the other story. What if we had known before the last series of scenes (once the characters are back on Moya) that it was quite likely Talyn had fired on his own? It would have created more tension and it's too bad that the writers took the lazy way out here with the secondary (B) story.

Crichton and Aeryn react within predictable limits. This episode didn't really do much to further their character development, although allowing them a moment alone at the end reinforces their relationship, whatever that may be at this point. Zaahn has some fine moments.

Notice how she manipulates the truth to try and build a bridge between the prisoners and their captors — something more obvious on subsequent viewings. Her relationship with Stark is also very nicely done. It's clear that they care for each other and that even before they shared Unity, he was drawn to her.

D'Argo is physically isolated from the others throughout most of the episode. Note how he's placed on the mushroom platform. He's often seen with his back to the others and one can almost feel the waves of anger coming off him. He's pissy with Crichton and openly hostile with Stark. This makes his conversation with Chiana all the more poignant. It also raises the question of whether or not they will be able to work through their differences. If D'Argo recognizes his own mistrust and tendency to be judgmental or place blame, perhaps losing Stark will be enough of a shock to not only examine his behavior, but change it as well.

And then we have Crais and Talyn. Although Crichton and D'Argo are open about distrusting Crais' motives, it doesn't seem to occur to anyone that Talyn might not be the nice lovable creature Aeryn and the others want him to be.

Talyn is Crais' secret project. He's been invested in it for some time — as we saw in "The Way We Weren't." There are some interesting and fascinating possibilities here and I'm curious to see which way the creative team will go.

For example, what if Crais was never really after Crichton, but used him as a cover in his search for Talyn? Crais' brother's death was certainly difficult, but what if — like B'Soog ("Home on the Remains") he is willing to sacrifice someone he loves to get something he wants. The gunship hybrid is an incredibly powerful weapon, more advanced than any Peacekeeper ship because it's a living entity -- one that is also theoretically, able to reproduce. Now that Crais has figured out how to breed these creatures, there's nothing to stop him from exploring that possibility.

Perhaps he used Scorpius as well — he certainly used Rygel and the others to further his own ambitions. Scorpius' single-minded pursuit of Crichton only helped Crais. He didn't really care about advancing in Peacekeeper ranks. He knew that he was an outlaw at the end of "That Old Black Magic" when he kills Lieutenant Teeg in order to prevent her from telling anyone that Central Command had demanded he break off his search for Crichton. But it wasn't Crichton he was looking for. It was Moya.

Gaining access to Moya in "Family Ties" and maintaining ties with Aeryn through "Mind the Baby" was brilliant strategy on Crais' part. He's no fool. He masterminded the breeding project. But he's slippery. He seems honorable one moment and then in the next he betrays his companions without a second thought. Personally, I think that Aeryn never really stood a chance of bonding with Talyn. Crais wanted to keep her around for several reasons -- first, she seemed to have some kind of bond with Talyn, though not one strong enough to ensure Tayln would offer Aeryn the Hand of Friendship (the neural interface). Second, it seems obvious that Crais is attracted to Aeryn given the once-over he gave her in "The Way We Weren't" and the way he interacts with her physically during much of the first season's four-episode arc finale. Separated from Crichton, Crais probably believes it's possible for him to win Aeryn over. To seduce her with the idea of bonding — with Talyn.

Aeryn seems completely unwilling to even examine the possibility that Talyn might actually be violent by nature. It's not something Crais wants to change. But he does need to figure out how to interact with Talyn effectively. I suspect that the deal with the Plokavians was simply a front to draw Moya and the crew into danger. Knowing that Talyn would fire on the Plokavian ship carrying forbidden cargo, Crais figured that at best, everyone would be captured and killed and at worst, the five members of Moya's crew to board Talyn would be eliminated. Moya and her crew are really the only ones who have full knowledge of Crais' movements, Talyn's potential, etc. Scorpius doesn't figure into the picture because Crais knows Scorpius is interested in wormhole technology, not leviathan hybrids.

Until the crew is willing to explore the possibility that Talyn is not the gentle leviathan that Moya is, they run the risk of putting themselves into mortal danger again and again. Crais is not going to stop until he gets what he wants. He has no reason to because he may well have the most powerful weapon in the Uncharted Territories. Now if he can only figure out how to fully utilize it's potential.

And THAT opens up some really intriguing possibilities. This is, ultimately, what saves the episode from being just another run of the mill scifi story because it contributes significantly to the story arc.

Grade: B+

Episode 10217: A Clockwork Nebari
Location: Close to a Nebari Base in the Uncharted Territories
Guest Cast:
Skye Wansey as Varla
Simon Bossell as Nerri
Malcolm Kennard as Meelak
Lani Tupu as Captain Bailar Crais
Wayne Pygram as Scorpius
Writer: Lily Taylor
Director: Rowan Woods

SYNOPSIS:

Although   Chiana   has   managed   to   procure

information about Jothee, she manages to get herself into trouble once again. In the docking bay, Crichton tells her that not only will D'Argo be unhappy with the way in which she got the information, but Aeryn is sure to give Chiana a piece of her mind when she returns as well. Chiana defends her tactics, even though Crichton calls her a "trollop."

When Aeryn returns to Moya, she is so relaxed it's actually frightening. And she's missing her pulse pistol. Rygel, equally as mellow, tells Chiana they have a present for her. One hopes that Aeryn kept the receipt, though, because Chiana will want to return the gift of a Nebari female named Varla who is bent on returning Chiana to Nebari Prime.

Aeryn and Varla go to Pilot's chamber to install a control collar on Pilot as the drug-induced mind-cleansing doesn't work on Pilot's race. The collar prevents Pilot from controlling many of Moya's systems and will also result in his death if Moya attempts to starburst away from the Nebari base that is Varla's destination. When Varla collapses from wounds sustained during an encounter with a Peacekeeper patrol, probaby from Scorpius' Command Carrier, Aeryn not only lovingly cradles the Nebari woman, but also stitches her wounds.

Joined a short time later by a Nebari male, Meelak, the crew are systematically mind-cleansed. Chained, collared and placed into a cell with Crichton and D'Argo, Chiana keeps insisting that she doesn't know why the Nebari want her so badly, but after D'Argo is taken away, she reveals more about her past.

She and Nerri, she says, did not escape from Nebari Prime. They were released, along with countless other young Nebari. It wasn't until two cycles later that she and Nerri realized why they were freed so easily: They were both infected with a contagion which is spread through sexual contact. Being young and adventuresome, Chiana ruefully admits that both she and Nerri certainly helped the Establishment spread their contagion. Nerri, though, is given an anti-body which rids him of the contagion. He shares the anti-body with Chiana who experiences excrutiating pain as the contagion works its way out of her system.

Nerri, because he can identify the person who provided the anti-body, decides that he must part company with Chiana after she recovers, even though she begs him not to leave her. That was, she tells Crichton, the last time she ever saw him.

Crichton is taken away to be cleansed and just before they pull his eyeballs out to install the device which will disperse the drug into his system, D'Argo feels it necessary to unburden himself. He apologizes profusely to Crichton for all of his impure thoughts and all the warrior-inspired deeds he's committed over the years. In a comic exchange in the face horror, Crichton assures D'Argo that they'll have a heart-to-heart male bonding moment ... later. Crichton's eyeballs are pulled from his head, the implant is attached to his optic nerve and he's pronounced cleansed.

Varla is convinced Chiana knows where Nerri is hiding. Chiana, thinking she's being played for a fool, tells Varla Nerri died nearly a quarter-cycle ago. But then Varla shows Chiana a recent vid of Nerri attacking a Nebari freight convoy. Chiana, elated but confused, tries to convince Varla that this new information doesn't change the fact that she still doesn't know where her brother is hiding.

Varla and Meelak explain that the contagion she helped spread will soon be activated. Because there were hundreds and maybe even thousands of Nebari who were released from Nebari Prime carrying the contagion, the number of infected species throughout this section of the Territories is astronomical. Once the contagion is active, chaos will ensue within the cultures who have infected members. This chaos, Meelak explains, will make it easier for the Nebari emissaries to establish contact — read domination — on these worlds.

In the meantime, while Zhaan, Aeryn and D'Argo are zoning out, Crichton gets several visions from Scorpius. He tells Crichton to fight the drug and Crichton realizes that he's free of the cleansing. When he tells Chiana this, she's not convinced at first that he's telling the truth. So he strikes her. They figure that overcoming the drug-induced cleansing must have to do with metabolism and Rygel, because he's an eating machine, probably has already purged the drug from his system.

Rygel, unfortunately, is the Dominar poster child for self-preservation and refuses to get involved. This riles Crichton enough to engage in a shouting match which draws Meelak's attention. Crichton, in a fit of very un-cleansed rage, punches Rygel and they leave him unconscious in the mess hall. Meelak and Crichton return to the holding cell where Chiana is still chained. There Meelak reveals that he's actually one of the good guys and shows Chiana a DNA-activated vid of Nerri.

Nerri is indeed alive and leading a resistance movement aimed at preventing the Establishement on Nebari from carrying out their evil plan of universal domination and cleansing. He also tells her (in characteristic Farscape mysogonistic terms) that the work is too dangerous for her to be involved with — as if living on the run from Scorpius is a cakewalk — and that she is not to join him. Meelak plans to take the Nebari transport ship as soon as they're in range of the station as he has important information to relay to Nerri, but refuses to take Chiana with him.

Meelak releases Crichton who proceeds to Pilot's chambers where they concoct a plan to try and fool both Nebari by staging a faked Peacekeeper attack. They hope, of course, that the diversion will allow them to overpower Varla. Because of the control collar, Pilot needs John's help to physically hardwire a new connection in Moya's neural cluster. And since there's no one else Crichton can turn to, he has to convince Rygel to help him. This proves difficult, but Aeryn's arrival gives Crichton the opening he needs to hustle Rygel away to Moya's neural cluster.

Aeryn is not convinced of John's mellow intentions, however, and she and D'Argo arrive in the neural cluster before Crichton has finished the modifications. Inspired by Rygel's playing with two live wires, Crichton manages to outwit Aeryn and D'Argo by shocking them. He hurries to Command, leaving D'Argo and Aeryn unconscious on the floor.

Chiana has managed to get both Varla and Meelak up to Command by telling them she'll cooperate, but until Crichton arrives, indicating the rewiring is complete, there is no image on the viewscreen to fool them and Varla is growing increasingly impatient.

The faked attack begins, complete with explosions. But despite their best efforts, they are unable to triumph, partly due to the fact that Meelak will not jeapordize his position with the resistance to aid Chiana or Crichton. Finally, however, he senses that Varla's desire for revenge has taken her beyond the boundaries of acceptable behavior and he kills her, claiming she has betrayed the intent of their mission. Why he doesn't do this earlier, however, is something of a mystery.

Control collars removed, D'Argo, Aeryn and Zhaan are penned up together in one holding cell while Rygel taunts them from the outside. Although it's clear that the drug has worn off, he doesn't seem in any hurry to let them out.

Chiana begs Meelak to take her with him to see Nerri, but he again refuses. Crichton arrives in the docking bay and gently reminds her that the success of the resistance actually depends upon her staying away from Nerri. Crichton tells her that knowing he is alive must be enough for now and as Meelak's ship departs, he draws her away.

CRITIQUE:

Writer Lily Taylor does an admirable job here of conveying a lot of information, but the script is uneven and relies too heavily on exposition. Despite this, however, there are some fine dramatic moments.

Had Taylor made better use of flashback or even some outside the box thinking regarding getting the information across to the audience, the episode would not have felt so talky in parts. For example, the connection between Nerri and Chiana had real depth in the flashback sequence, but not enough to cement the true nature of their bond. Though Chiana says they were granted exit visas when they were young and this scene takes place two cycles after they'd left Nebari Prime, Chiana did not look any younger. What kind of a timeline are we to infer from this? How many cycles has it been since they left Nebari Prime?

The conversation Chiana has with Crichton which includes this sequence is extremely hard to follow the first time, mostly because of the bad sound. Ms. Edgley was not adequately mic-ed given the way the director has instructed her to play Chiana and huge chunks of the dialogue are muddy.

The explanation of the Nebari plan for domination and the re-stating of the way the drug removes violent or other "inappropriate" impulses are two examples of places where the script editing could have been better. Some of the repitition could be the result of the editing as there are usually several scenes which are shot and never used or even several scenes spliced together to make one. But the exposition throughout the episode really slowed the pacing.

One way to cope with the amount of information we needed to understand the complexity of the Establishement's plan and the resistance would have been to make use of a montage during the exposition. A series of images featuring Nerri and Chiana, for example, would have helped deepen the audience's sense of their closeness while underscoring the numerous worlds they've visited and unknowingly infected with the contagion. Money, of course, is always a factor and it's certainly cheaper to have three characters standing and talking than it is to create this kind of sequence.

One has to wonder, however, with the show's enormous popularity why more of the profit isn't being funnelled back into the production — especially in terms of sound and costuming. These poor folks have been wearing the same clothes for nearly a year. And it's damn hard to find a good dry-cleaner for leather in the Uncharted Territories.

There were several other issues I had with the script as well. First, why not use the spinal column or the brainstem as a way to get the drug into one's system? Using the optic nerve seemed unrealistic, just a way to get in a good gross-out scene. And I had to wonder whether it was actually possible to pull one's eyeballs from the socket and let them pop back in without causing permanent damage to both the organ and the nerves. It just didn't seem like a very good idea, especially given the fact that the treatments have to be continuously administered. After a while, everyone would go around looking like a bad Halloween mask with their eyeballs hanging half-way down their cheeks.

And if Pilot's control collar actually pierced the flesh, why didn't the Nebari use this method to inject the drug? Or did they? This wasn't very clear. Was the collar a back-up device just in case the drug didn't work? Why bother with the drug at all if the collar causes such intense pain, especially since so many species seem immune to the drug's effects?

Was Durka's metabolism that different from Aeryn's? Why was he able to metabolize the drug when she wasn't? Was Crichton only able to overcome the drug because of the possible chip in his brain, courtesy of Scorpius?

If the Nebari Establishment knows that those they send out into the Territories will be promiscuous, why does everyone see Chiana as a slut? She says both she and Nerri unwittingly helped the Establishement — and the implication here was the she wasn't the only one getting laid on a regular basis. Why must the creative team persist in hammering this point home by having Crichton call her a tramp in the opening teaser?

It seems that — the Nebari are sluts then — why else would a government use a sexually transmitted contagion? And if this is the case, then can't we argue that Chiana's sex drive is genetic? Or perhaps the Establishment altered her when they gave her the contagion, lowering her inhibitions, manipulating other factors which would encourage her and the others to act on their impulses and urges. What if they culled out the brightest and most rebellious and free-thinking of their race, altered and infected them and then sent them off-world? The fact that the Establishment has thought this through enough to have created the contagion in the first place is enough, as far as I'm concerned, to give credence to these questions. And that said, I wish the creative team would just let Chiana be who she is without constantly demeaning her actions.

The fact that she tells John the truth about her past and not D'Argo again seems to point to the relationship ending. There seems to be no connection between D'Argo and Chiana in this episode though John is quick to remind her that D'Argo won't be pleased with how she obtained the information about Jothee.

In terms of pronunciation and spelling, if Nebari is pronounced Neh-bar-ee, and Meelak is pronounced Me-lack, why is Nerri pronounced Near-ee and not Nehr-ee?

Zhaan, who has been the medic on board up to this point, does not treat Varla's wounds. The fact that Aeryn stitches up Varla seems out of character for her. What was the point of having Aeryn practically fondle Varla in Pilot's chamber? If she's so relaxed and mellow, why doesn't she come on to John? If one imagines the drug might act like a good stiff drink or some of the proverbial Maui Wowie (note John's surfer-dude facade), why does Aeryn cozy up to a Nebari woman she doesn't even know? Was that one of those ratings-ploy male fantasies — let's see Aeryn get it on (implied though it was) with another woman?

And speaking of Varla, why was the flesh around the wound Aeryn stitched blue, but the cuts on her face red? Is their flesh blue or red? If their blood is dark blue, then it seems their skin would not appear red or pink, even when damaged, but dark blue or grey or even black.

John makes a big deal about the fact that he's afraid Rygel will electrocute them when they're hardwiring in Moya's neural cluster. But then he doesn't hesitate to zap both D'Argo and Aeryn to the point where D'Argo is convulsing on the floor. Wouldn't a dose of power that strong kill both D'Argo and Aeryn?

John's anger management is really getting bad here. In fact, he's bordering on abusive. He punches Rygel in the face when Rygel won't cooperate with him. He punches Chiana in the face when she is hesitant to believe his claim that he's overcome the drug. He seems more than willing to nearly kill his best friend and would-be lover. Crichton hasn't been portrayed as this kind of macho warrior guy. D'Argo has always been the one to punch first and ask questions later. I'm worried that the creative team has become lazy and allows him to simply hit rather than use his brain as he's done in the past. I'm not a big fan of this kind of violence, as it certainly doesn't provide much of an example of decent adult behavior. And although television has never been at the forefront of presenting positive role models from young viewers, this show's demographics are diverse enough that it's worth considering. Personally, I abhor seeing men hit women.

Even D'Argo wouldn't strike Aeryn who is, in essence, a fellow warrior. Seeing Crichton punch Chiana was more than a little disconcerting and in truth, there were other ways to handle this scene.

Chiana is a fascinating character and the Nebari a powerful and frightening race. I hope that the creative team will revisit this storyline as there are many unanswered questions. How will the contagion emerge? What kind of cultural chaos will result? Are the emissaries already hovering about waiting for the day of their imagined glory to arrive? How is the resistance organized? What is their plan? What is the connection between Nerri and the person who provided him with the antigen? All intriguing questions -- all worth more screen time.

What works in this show is the powerful AIDS metaphor, the shame Chiana feels at being used by her government and the performances by both Ms. Edgley and Mr. Browder. Although Crichton doesn't get to stretch much here, the scenes between John and Chiana (aside from the punching sequence) are very well done. The fondness these two characters feel for each other is palpable. He really does empathize with her desire to see Nerri and the impossibility of that desire being realized.

Grade: B

Episode 10218: Liars, Guns and Money Part 1: A Not So Simple Plan
Location: The Shadow Depository in the Uncharted Territories
Guest Cast:
Wayne Pygram as Scorpius
Paul Goddard as Stark
David Franklin as Lt. Braca
Claudia Karvan as Natira
Matt Newton as Jothee
Adrian Brown as Gan

Jennifer Fisher as PK Nurse
Writer: Grant McAloon
Director: Andrew Prowse

SYNOPSIS:

This first of three parts begins in media res. Zhaan, insisting that Stark's mask has spoken to her, wants Moya to continue on the course he proscribed. D'Argo adamantly wants to turn around and go back toward the slave auctions in the hopes of saving Jothee.

Just as Zhaan asks Crichton his opinion, Stark's face appears within the mask and he urges them forward. Pilot alerts the crew to a ship close by with a desperately weak life sign aboard – Stark.

Before he's barely strong enough to speak, Stark is telling D'Argo about a fool-proof plan for obtaining enough money to purchase Jothee, who's going to be sold in a lot of ten thousand slaves. The plan involves robbing a high security depository where supposed criminals store their wealth. When Crichton and the others express concern not only over stealing someone else's wealth but also breaking into a fortress which Aeryn points out has more weaponry than the Gammak base, D'Argo calls them all cowards.

In typical D'Argo fashion, he ignores the common sense warnings of his crewmates and takes one of the transport pods to the depository. Crichton and Aeryn go after him. Crichton thinks he sees Scorpius, but it turns out it's only a hallucination. As he's realizing this, D'Argo begins hacking into the security system. Trying to create a diversion, Crichton engages one of the guards by claiming he has all eleven secret ingredients for KFC. But D'Argo is caught anyway.

He's taken away to be interrogated and Crichton and Aeryn return to Moya, furious. They go after Stark; Crichton physically attacks him. But Stark assures him that it's all part of the plan. Stark claims that he can break into the depository's security system while they're changing their security codes — but it has to be within the next six arns. He tries to shoo Crichton away and then says that D'Argo thinks Crichton is just a lazy bum. Crichton calls Stark on the lie and Stark backs down.

In the meantime, Zhaan, Chiana and Rygel are preparing for their part in this excursion. Zhaan has concocted a gas which will render Rygel's lifesigns unreadable. While she and Chiana pose as potential depositors, Rygel will be entombed within one of the containers. When the gas wears off, he'll use an electronic device to swap containers and theoretically, no one will be the wiser.

Zhaan, wearing a fetching black leather ensemble complete with eye patch and skullcap, manages to convince Natira that not only was D'Argo part of her plan, but she also has a very expensive cargo that she needs to store for one solar day. Natira is the depository's chief of security and deposits. She also seems to have some unusual talents for persuading individuals to reveal information which she uses to get D'Argo to tell her his name.

D'Argo is released and Chiana accompanies him back to Moya. Crichton and Aeryn, who have come along to act as guards, are ushered to a room where they can watch the procedure. While Zhaan is completing the transaction with Natira, Scorpius shows up to claim his possessions. It's clear that the staff know him — and fear him. He overpowers Natira's primary assistant and misses seeing Zhaan by a matter of microts.

Natira is eager to placate Scorpius, especially once he surmises that she's confiscated his possessions after hearing rumors of his demise. When he insists the payback be three times the worth of what he deposited, she reluctantly agrees. Then she spends some time making it up to him in other ways, which mostly involve licking his eyeball and leather nose piece.

Back on Moya, D'Argo is recovering slowly and he and Crichton have a bit of a go about whether or not they should have gotten into this in the first place. This annoys Chiana and she berates Crichton. But the tension between the two men is rising and although it's clear that Crichton thinks this is all a very bad idea, he understands D'Argo's motivation.

Crichton is also beginning to have a bad feeling about Stark. When Crichton confronts Stark about the motivation behind his plan, Stark confesses that he knew that Scorpius had a storage container at this depository and that he was motivated by revenge against Scorpius. Crichton, becoming more and more furious as the plan becomes more complex and dangerous, asks Zhaan to concoct a gel that will increase heat. It's clear he plans to spread this on the cold rods that Scorpius inserts in his head.

When Zhaan returns to the depository to withdraw her cargo, Crichton and Aeryn find Scorpius by using the security cameras. Crichton is unable to smear the new cold rod with the gel, so Aeryn does it for him. She finishes microts before the PK girl who is Scorpius' assistant comes to retrieve the rods and lands on top of Crichton behind a couch. Aside from Rygel's nearly bungled attempt to switch containers, it's the episode's only moment of comic relief.

At this point, as one would expect, it all starts to go wrong. The container Rygel has swapped for their own is the one Natira has earmarked for Scorpius. She recognizes the strange sculpture that housed the "dead" Rygel and when she describes the rest of the companions, Scorpius knows immediately who is behind this plan.

He commands Natira to seal off the doors. She wrestles briefly with him for the upper hand, but backs down when he reminds her of how much she owes him. If he leaves with Crichton, Scorpius says, he will call their debt even.

Aboard Moya, D'Argo has returned to command to

find Stark on the verge of a nervous breakdown. He manages to jam the security cameras briefly, but trying to guide two separate parties out of the depository proves impossible. Crichton, trapped with Aeryn in one corridor, finally convinces him to open up all the doors. He and Aeryn head toward the transport area in the hopes of catching up with Zhaan, Chiana and Rygel.

Stark finally loses control and smashes the panel he's been using to inferface with the depository's security system. The three-dimensional image goes blank. D'Argo, in a desperate race to get the system back online before his crewmates are caught, finally manages to reconnect. In the meantime, Zhaan uses a second dose of her knock-out gas to disable the security personnel who catch up with them (giving herself and Chiana an anti-knock out pill, but not Rygel). Aeryn and Crichton meet up with them. Crichton stays behind to secure the other doors.

Just as he thinks he'll get away, Scorpius appears and grabs Crichton by the throat. He admits that he did implant a chip into Crichton's head – which proves to John that he's not crazy. The heat gel in Scorpius' head begins to take effect; the PK girl assistant removes it and it explodes in her face, killing her. Now Scorpius needs Crichton to implant the new rod, using language reminiscent of the "Give it to me" scene from Falling Down. Using the chip and his own will power, he struggles against Crichton's hatred and refusal. Finally Crichton tells Scorpius that he's not Crichton's type and breaks away. The scene ends with Scorpius reaching for the cold rod, which is just out of his grasp.

Reunited on Moya, D'Argo pledges his friendship to Stark, but Chiana reminds him that Crichton, too, was crucial in making the plan work and yet D'Argo will not speak to him. Zhaan and Stark share an intimate moment in the middle of Rygel and Chiana fingering their new-found wealth. And off to the side, Crichton sits alone. Aeryn joins him. He believes that Scorpius is dead and is troubled over the fact that he still feels connected to his enemy.

Then he broaches the subject of his feelings for her, which he'd done once before in the middle of their escape. She repeats to him that she understands and that he doesn't have to say anything. Gently, she draws his head to her shoulder.

Later, something emerges from one of the cargo containers. It's metallic. It has legs. It looks like some kind of nasty spider. And part one of this trilogy ends.

CRITIQUE:

After a long break, the return of Farscape is a much anticipated event. And this episode both rewards and disappoints. First, let's look at what works. Zhaan. Ah, the sight of Zhaan in leather is hauntingly erotic. As with Aeryn, the dichotomy of femininity and masculinity is engaging. Finally, she's shed her priestess robes (which this season were not particularly flattering) and taken on the robes of someone used to getting her way. She's sized up by Natira, and spooked by her once – when the cargo container first comes barreling down the shoot and into the secure room, it looks as though it will kill both of them. Natira, having been through this procedure before, doesn't flinch. Zhaan does. B ut only the first time. Due to the editing/directing choices, however, the near-impact of the container isn't as powerful as it might have been. Personally, I would have shifted to the side-view of the room a bit sooner to show the container entering rather than showing it moving through the shoot. Yes, we can tell it's coming fast, but the cut to the shoot is choppy and the shock effect is lessened.

In an episode that is very much an ensemble piece, Zhaan's performance and the role she's asked to play stand out. Finally, we get to see both the character and the actor stretch. She's been terribly underused this season. I suspect it's because the creative team is focusing too much on the demographic who want Chiana as their bed-mate. Zhaan is just as sensual, just as erotic and just as interesting. Clearly, no one there has really thought about the appeal of a more mature, more experienced, woman. Perhaps this will change in Season 3.

Rygel, up to his usual tricks, is merely part of the equation, as is Pilot. Aeryn and Crichton share a couple of moments which begin to explore the deepening of their relationship, but it's really the plot here which is the focus.

Neither Chiana nor D'Argo grow much in this episode. D'Argo's story arc is so clearly drawn that there's nothing else on his mind. As Mr. Simcoe has said several times in interviews, he approaches D'Argo's character as though the Luxan were a teenager. Thus, his impulsive responses to situations, his lack of experience in warfare and interpersonal relationships, his disdain for authority – unless he's in charge – are all right on the mark. Even though D'Argo's chronological age has been established as thirty-something, it's clear, as Zhaan said early on, that he is hardly more than a boy.

It must be frustrating for Crichton, especially, as his desire for adult male companionship is not met in D'Argo and even less so in Stark.

Stark. Now here is an interesting character that the writers can't seem to agree how to play. His role here leaves the viewer with nothing but questions. If he can recombine his molecules to exist on this plane, why does he come back in the same nasty clothes and the same unwashed body? If he can recreate himself, why was he a slave? Why was he a prisoner? If he can recombine, why couldn't he un-combine to escape Scorpius' torture? This question, of course, leads to another. At one point, Crais mentions that Stark's race is a slave race – how can this be? They seem too evolved on some level to have fallen prey to slavery. What kind of backstory would address this?

And why would he be so excited about becoming rich? He's almost ecstatic about the idea of wealth which runs in direct contrast to the way he's been portrayed in past episodes. Zhaan seems to be totally taken with him. This only makes sense in terms of his past interactions with her, particularly sharing Unity, but his behavior here is so base that it raises the question of what she sees in him that is not adequately addressed.

This is the major problem aspect of this episode. The other problems are small, but annoying. For example, the use of words like "bank" and "blueprints" don't seem to fit with this universe, despite the translator microbes. Why is it necessary for Chiana to confirm that a depository is a bank? Did the writer think the audience wouldn't get it? Scorpius dismisses his PK assistant – the one who changes his rods for him – and then she's suddenly back two scenes later. How many transport pods did they take to the depository? If Chiana accompanies D'Argo back to Moya, and the prowler only seats two, then how did Zhaan return? Can she fly a pod? Can Chiana? This hasn't been established. If the containers are linked to the depositor's genetic profile, as Natira assures Zhaan, then how did the crew open the ones they stole? And if they have no money to begin with, where do they come up with the funds to pay for the deposit?

Fine pacing and a cliff-hanger ending make the episode worth watching. Additionally some inspired camera work and fantastic set design only deepen our appreciation of the Farscape universe.

Grade: B

Episode 10219: Liars, Guns and Money Part 2: With Friends Like These
Location: Aboard Moya and at the Shadow Depository
Guest Cast:
Wayne Pygram as Scorpius

Paul Goddard as Stark
David Franklin as Lt Braca
Claudia Karvan as Natira
Matt Newton as Jothee
Nicholas Hope as Akkor
Thomas Holgrove as Teurac
John Adam as Bekhesh
Jeremy Sims as Rorf
Jo Kerrigan as Rorg
David Wheeler as Durka
David Bowers as Kurz
Writer: Naren Shankar
Director: Catherine Millar

SYNOPSIS:

The episode opens with Rygel bemoaning the fleeting taste of wealth. Although he's afraid there won't be anything left over for himself after Jothee and the other slaves are purchased, Chiana is optimistic about her small share and reveals that she plans to buy some special silk for her bed. Rygel does not seem surprised.

Just before they reach the destination point, D'Argo asks Aeryn if she thinks Jothee will remember him and whether he did the right thing by sending Jothee away. Aeryn assures him that Jothee would be dead now if D'Argo had not sent him away, as PK's despise halfbreeds. When they reach the Katan mines, they find out that the slave lot of which Jothee was a part has already been sold to a special buyer for triple the price. Their worst fears are confirmed when a message from Scorpius confirms that he has Jothee and will only trade him for Crichton.

Intense anger erupts among the crew. Crichton goes after Stark, realizing that Scorpius managed to access Stark's console during the robbery and this is how Scorpius determined their true objective. D'Argo can barely contain his fury at Crichton for hesitating when the subject of the burglary was first proposed. Crichton's lack of enthusiam, D'Argo believes, is what has caused their delay and also the date of the auction. D'Argo storms off to his quarters where has an imaginary conversation with his son. Jothee challenges him — saying that D'Argo knows how to get him back, but is afraid.

At the Shadow Depository, Scorpius gets the bad news that the slavers won't look through ten thousand slaves for one Luxan. Natira and her assistant propose that they resell the other slaves to recoup their losses. He tells her that the money is her problem and dispatches Lt. Braca to bring the Luxan to the Shadow Despository.

Back on Moya, Pilot tells Aeryn that there are several places where Moya is exhibiting metal fatigue. She instructs the DRDs to take a sample. When she's joined by Crichton, he optimistically says he has a plan to save Jothee.

In command, Crichton tells the crew he believes Scorpius will bring Jothee to the Shadow Depository. Crichton proposes they link up with some of the individuals they've come into contact with in the past to help them rescue the boy. Since they no longer need the money to buy the slave lot, they can pay mercenary soldiers, including the Vorcarian Blood-Trackers, a fire-spewing Sheyang and a gauntlet-wearing Tevlek, to help them.

Just before they set off on their separate missions, Stark collapses, screaming. He claims that he has just heard the cries of the dying Bannack slaves as they're killed on the freighter.

Scorpius, afraid that Crichton is forming some kind of plan to rescue Jothee, is enraged when he's informed that there will be a delay in delivering Jothee. Natira admonishes Scorpius for losing his temper, afraid he'll blow out his cooling rods. He informs her that he's upgraded his system several times since they first met. She's confused by his preoccupation with Crichton and when Scorpius claims it's because Crichton destroyed the Gammak base, she questions him, but he reveals nothing more. Although she admits that he's not as volatile as he was when she took him in some time ago — and he reminds her that he saved her life — she is still taken with him and there is definitely a sexual chemistry between them.

When Rygel discovers Chiana helping herself to a little extra profit, they discover that one of the crates is empty. A moment later Chiana falls though to the tier below and discovers that their money has legs and is eating the ship.

Crichton, in the Farscape 1, arrives at Tevlek Bekhesh's lodging and comes upon him in the midst of morning prayer. Crichton knocks him unconscious, but then realizes that Bekhesh doesn't have the gauntlet. During one raid, Bekhesh tells Crichton, he captured and killed a holy man. He kept the Writ of Taru the priest carried with him and because of this has given up his life of violence. Crichton binds him and soon enough the Tavlek's need for the drug in the gauntlet causes him to reveal its location.

Crichton just wants to take it for himself, but Bekhesh claims he won't last longer than three arns as the dosage has been increased three-fold since their last encounter. Reluctantly, Crichton agrees to let Bekhesh accompany him back to Moya.

On Moya, Pilot tells Zhaan that the money creatures are devouring Moya's sense filaments, causing her intense pain. Additionally they're eating through the metal at an alarming rate, so a hull breach seems imminent. Zhaan analyzes one of the creatures that Chiana manages to capture and they realize to their dismay that the only way to kill them is through exposing them to intense heat.

Meanwhile, Aeryn approaches a Sheyang vessel. When they don't respond to her hail, she boards to find the ship all but abandoned. The lone Sheyang commander, Teurac, is willing to help her, but he's almost too weak to be of any use. He convinces her that he'll recover and climbs back into the prowler with Aeryn to return to Moya.

D'Argo comes upon the Vorcarian Blood-Trackers and saves them from being killed by PK mercinaries. They tell him Rorg is with child and so they'd broken off their pursuit of PK deserters but kept half the money. They agree to help D'Argo find his son. Although Rorf is reluctant to leave his mate, she reminds him they owe D'Argo a debt. It is because of him that their children will survive. Rorg agrees to go to nearby caves to await the birth of their offspring while Rorg accompanies D'Argo back to Moya.

While Zhaan struggles against the knowledge that the only way to kill the infestation is to burn them out, Scorpius contacts Moya. With Jothee clearly visible in the background, he demands to talk with Crichton and D'Argo. Zhaan stalls. Stark pushes her aside and taunts him to kill the boy. How could you kill so many Bannack slaves, he demands, for one Luxan! Go ahead, he says, kill the boy because not only does he mean nothing to Stark, but he also will not exchange Crichton for Jothee.

Stunned, Zhaan and the others turn on Stark, but he assures them Scorpius won't kill Jothee. They agree to trust him. For now.

When Jothee arrives at the Shadow Depository, he's brought before Scorpius. Wondering what kind of a creature Scorpius is, Natira says that Scorpius is the product of the rape of a Sebacean woman by a Scarran. When Scorpius asks if the boy has any loyalties to either the Sebaceans or the Luxans, Jothee only says that his uncle killed his mother.

As Moya nears the Flax, Rygel departs to approach the Zenetian pirates only to discover that Captain Kcrackek is dead and Durka has assumed his place. Terrified, Rygel still tries to negotiate with Durka, but Durka merely threatens him. So Rygel stabs him.

Back on Moya, Zhaan and Chiana disperse the

flammable gas which will kill the creatures. Knowing there's no other way to rid Moya of the infestation, they ignite the gas inside Moya. The pain in excruciating. Pilot allows Zhaan and Stark to share Moya's pain.

When Crichton arrives with the Tavlek, he's terrified to see part of Moya in flames, but Chiana reassures him that everyone is all right. Everyone, that is, except Moya. The damage is extensive and the pain so intense that Moya cannot starburst. While Crichton and Aeryn survey the damaged tiers, Zhaan weeps for the pain she's inflicted and their loss. And now, with no money to pay the mercenaries, it seems there will be problems. Just when it seems the mercenaries will kill each other and the crew, Rygel shows up with Durka's head and tells everyone that if they don't cooperate, they'll end up like Durka.

As plans are being made for the attack on the Shadow Depository, no one can find Crichton. At that moment, a figure descends the stairs. D'Argo turns to find Jothee. They share an emotional reunion. When Aeryn asks how Jothee escaped, he tells them he was simply freed. The terrible realization that Crichton has traded himself for Jothee sinks in.

At the Shadow Depository, Scorpius surveys Crichton with glee.

CRITIQUE:

This episode really maintains the tension and questions raised in the first part of this three-part story. The pacing is excellent and the balance among stories is nicely handled.

In terms of character development, the writers have backed Crichton into the proverbial corner. He really doesn't have many choices open to him and it's not surprising that he agrees to trade himself for Jothee. The chip in his head is interfering more and more with his daily life. As with Crais' pursuit in Season 1, Scorpius' constant presence is really beginning to take its toll.

It seems reasonale to expect that the crew will go after Crichton as they have done in the past. Perhaps this gesture will finally create the bond between D'Argo and Crichton that Crichton so desires. It will be interesting to see where the creative team takes this storyline. Will Jothee's presence be the wedge that drives Chiana and D'Argo apart? Will being a parent mellow D'Argo?

And speaking of being a parent, if D'Argo is thirty cycles old and Jothee is presented as a teenager just how old was D'Argo when he fathered the boy? Is this usual in Luxan culture? Are their life spans shorter than other humanoid species in this part of the universe? Some interesting questions about Luxan culture are raised here which hopefully will be answered as the series progresses.

The map "problem" rears its ugly head here again when Pilot says he's been keeping track of where they've been as well as he can. Amazingly enough, Crichton is able to find the Tavlek; D'Argo the Blood Trackers and Aeryn the Sheyang all in the space of some two solar days. Find them, convince them to help and return. Moya has used starburst a number of times since each of these encounters and yet, miraculously, she can locate everyone right away — and find the Flax again — but in other similar situations, she can't seem to find her way out of a paper bag.

Bringing the mercenaries back into the picture is a treat for die-hard fans who will understand the references and have a deeper appreciation of the effect these characters have on the larger story arc. However, this plot device is just too convenient.

Stark, too, continues to be a problem. The creative team can't seem to decide whether he's an ally or a threat and it seems that in every single scene he's been directed by a different person. More than any other character, Stark suffers from the television and film industry's practice of shooting episodes vastly out of sequence. What's sacrificed here is a sense of continuity, especially in terms of this character.

Chiana's accent is also terribly uneven. In this episode, she sounds American, other times, Australian. It would be nice if the powers that be would make up their minds about how they want to play her and stop worrying about which demographics the accent will most appeal to. Personally, I prefer Ms. Edgley's natural "accent" rather than the flatness that the director has given to her so-called American tones.

In terms of the living money, I was confused as to why flushing them into the vacuum of space was not an option. While it was made clear that they could survive, it was not made clear whether or not Moya would still be infected by them from the outside. This clarification would have been helpful, especially given the terrible pain they had to inflict on her to rid her of the little beasties. Were they afraid that the critters would go about attacking other vessels? Why not let them loose on the metal buildings of the Shadow Depository itself? A bit more time on this would have left fewer red herrings.

On the positive side, this episode provides some fascinating information about Scorpius. The fact that he's the offspring of a Scarran and a Sebacean was revealed in Look at the Princess, but here we find out that Scorpius Sebacean mother was raped. Additionally, although the Sebaceans seem very dedicated to keeping their bloodlines pure, this is not the first time this has happened and in many cases the offspring are murdered to prevent further "contamination."

It was clear from part one of this arc that Natira and Scorpius had past history, and we learn more about that here, too, although some tantalizing bits are still missing. When Natira tells Scorpius he is not the hot-headed individual she took in years ago, it raises some fascinating questions about Scorpius' past. Was he abandoned by his mother? If so, who raised him? If not, how did she keep him from being killed by PK troops? Was she a Peacekeeper or a civilian? Is he the product of a conquering force? Would explain some of the hatred between the two races?

The fact that Scorpius and Natira's sexual encounter does not involve penetration -- at least this one did not — is actually not that unusual or uncommon. Consider the Klingon race, for example, from the Star Trek universe. Worf's marriage to a human woman was unusual, partly because of the intense pain rituals which accompany coupling. And although Jadzia Dax was tall and broad-shouldered, Dax' next host, Ezri, was downright tiny. When Worf and Ezri acknowledge the attraction that lies between them and have sex, one has to wonder how the Klingon could take a human lover, especially one of Ezri's build, and not actually cause her physical damage.

This ground has been covered elsewhere in scifi and interestingly enough, the most common explanation of how these seemingly disparate physical pairings would work often has to do with separating lovemaking from reproductive sex. Lovemaking, as we saw several times during the Jadzia/Worf relationship, often involved broken bones and deep muscle bruises. Reproductive sex would fall into a different realm altogether, one that would protect the mother-to-be from internal damage.

This, of course, was not a consideration for the Scarran who was Scorpius' father, but would be a factor in the interaction between Scorpius and Natira. His intense pleasure at taking of her sharp talon-like protrusions into his mouth openly suggest that not all bipeds in the Farscape universe experience sexual pleasure in the same ways. Remember Zhaan trying to seduce Rygel to her side in "DNA Mad Scientist" by stroking his eyebrows?

In general, this was a fine episode and a very strong middle piece, particularly when compared to the very weak middle section of the Look at the Princess trilogy.

Grade: A-

Episode 10220: Liars, Guns and Money Part 3: Plan B

Location: Aboard Moya and at the Shadow Depository
Guest Cast:
Wayne Pygram as Scorpius
Paul Goddard as Stark
David Franklin as Lt Braca
Claudia Karvan as Natira
Matt Newton as Jothee
Nicholas Hope as Akkor
Thomas Holgrove as Teurac
John Adam as Bekhesh
Jeremy Sims as Rorf
David Bowers as Kurz
Writer: Justin Mojo
Director: Tony Tilse

SYNOPSIS:

Scorpius has Crichton. Strapped on top of a metallic sphere, Crichton waits for Scorpius to remove the chip in his head. Scorpius claims that the chip, not Crichton's desire to save Jothee, brought Crichton to him.

Aboard Moya, the crew and their newly-hired mercenaries listen to Crichton's vid message. The message confirms what they had suspected: He's exchanged himself for Jothee.

Aeryn tries to convince everyone that their mission hasn't changed — only their objective. Logan, one of the Zenetian pirates points out the main problem — there are no longer any funds with which to pay them. He pulls his weapon and claims that Moya now belongs to him.

Aeryn, disgusted, tells the pirates that there's a huge flaw in their logic. The Shadow Depository is chocked full of riches beyond anyone's imagining. All they have to do is get in. The pirates are hesitant. Just at the point where it looks as though the pirates will win the argument and shoot Chiana, Jothee and Stark burst into Command demanding to know what's going on.

When Logan grabs Chiana and Rorg grabs Jothee, Stark loses control and berates them all for their selfishness, pointing out that nearly ten thousand of his people were slaughtered by Scorpius and they're arguing about payment.

Pilot breaks in with a message. There's a ship approaching: It's Talyn and Crais.

Responding to Moya's call for help, Talyn managed to find Moya. He is able to provide her with nutrients which will help the injured leviathan heal. As Aeryn and Crais walk through the burned-out decks, she tells him that eight entire tiers are damaged. Talyn will remain linked to Moya for two arns. Aeryn tries to enlist Crais' help — and Talyn's. Crais, taking an opportunity to lecture Aeryn about the futility of using violence and their claim that they did not want to use Talyn for violent purposes, refuses to lend his help. He tells Aeryn that Crichton is already dead, so it's pointless.

Back in command, Stark tries to explain an incredibly complicated plan to the mercenaries. Everyone has complaints and mistrust nearly brings everyone to blows once again.

In D'Argo's quarters, Jothee examines D'Argo's qualta blade. D'Argo arrives and says the blade was carried by his paternal grandfather at the Siege of Rakman. Jothee is impressed as the weapon is quite heavy. When D'Argo asks Jothee who scarred his face, Jothee tells him D'Argo is responsible, not only for the scars, but for everything that hass happened to him since D'Argo sent him away. Jothee, scarred by ten years of violence and self-preservation, doesn't want to participate in Crichton's rescue. He's afraid of losing the freedom he's just regained.

Down on the planet, Natira seems to be getting bored with the amount of time and energy Scorpius is putting into his Crichton project. She says he doesn't seem like a very interesting species and clearly she doesn't understand the importance of what's in Crichton's mind. Scorpius tells her he has to make sure Crichton's neural receptors are ready to have the probe removed -- and that his implant, which functions like another scifi device called a brainworm — has done its job.

Crichton tells Natira that what Scorpius really wants is to meet, greet and kill new cultures. She is clearly shocked and intrigued, but Scorpius, intent as he is on Crichton, does not see her sudden interest. He blithely counters by telling Crichton that he has no desire to rule the universe, but he does desire the power that the wormhole technology will bring him — and those he's allied with.

Scorpius goes into Crichton's memory. They're out on a dock in Sawyer's Mill, a place where Jack Crichton used to take John fishing. There are actually two Scorpius' inside Crichton's brain — one that is a manifestation of the neural plug (a.k.a. the brainworm) and has been looking for the information, and the other that is Scorpius' consciousness' manifestation in Crichton's mind.

True to character, Scorpius tells Crichton he won't free him once Scorpius has obtained the wormhole information, but will kill him once they're both aboard the Command Carrier. He stabs Crichton in the back of the neck. Crumpling to the ground, Crichton realizes he's still conscious, but paralyzed.

Aboard Talyn, Aeryn tells Crais that he can have anything he wants if he agrees to help them. Crais counters, asking Aeryn if she's offering herself in exchange for Crichton. She tells him he can take whatever he wants; she won't stop him.

Jothee, not wanting D'Argo to think he's a coward, agrees to help D'Argo free Crichton. They're interrupted by the mercenaries who want to discuss the plan -- again. Annoyed, D'Argo has Pilot tell the hired help that if they try to mutiny, Pilot will flood the maintenance bay with a gas that will render everyone unconscious. Logan, speaking for the others, says he has no desire to be killed, but even D'Argo must admit that the plan is deeply flawed. D'Argo agrees. He asks Pilot of Moya is well enough to perform a low atmosphere maneuver which will provide a distraction while they burst in through the main doors. Aeryn arrives and asks if everyone is ready. Logan asks what they'll do if Crichton is damaged beyond repair and Aeryn answers that she'll simply kill him.

At the Depository, Scorpius is informed that the Command Carrier has arrived six arns ahead of schedule. Scorpius is suspicious of this so-called good news, but before he has a chance to pursue this line of thought, his cooling rods give out and he finds himself in terrible pain. He leaves the chamber, instructing Natira to lock down the chamber and open it for no one but him.

Crichton goads Natira, telling her that she should come into his mind and see just how Scorpius plans to kill her. Angered, she punches him in the mouth and then tastes his blood.

The rescue plan is not going well. Rorf can't seem to find Crichton and Behkesh tells Pilot it's because smelling is the female Blood-Tracker's responsibility. Rorf and Bekhesh argue and then separate

Zhaan comes upon Turek trying to make fire, but he's having trouble. He tells her that although he still has the nutrients necessary to make flames, he can't tap into his nutrient store unless he has taka serum, which Zhaan tells him is poison.

Back at the Depository, Rorf is able to inform Pilot that Crichton is one level up from the main chamber before he's discovered by Akor, captured and tied to the same globe as Crichton. When Scorpius tries to get information out of him, he's unsuccessful. He claims that he is only casing the Depository for the Zenetian pirates. Natira uses her feminine ways to convince him by sprouting a set of nasty metal tentacles out of her head. When he still refuses to cooperate, she blinds him in one eye. Defeated, Rorf tells Scorpius everything.

When they realize that their plan has fallen apart, the crew and their hired help board the transport pod to try another approach. Teurec, Zhaan and Stark will go after the genenerators while D'Argo and Aeryn search for Crichton. Jothee will stay aboard the transport with Rygel, ready to pick them up.

Pilot, Chiana and one of the pirates fly low and close, shattering the glass around Crichton's chamber. This diversion makes it possible for Rygel to land the transport pod. While Scorpius tries to secure the generator with Akkor he sends Braca up to the monitor room. In the meantime, Crichton tries to convince Natira to free him. Since she's told him that the chip can be removed without killing him, he promises her the wormhole technology if she'll let him go.

Aeryn and D'Argo hook up with Behkesh and storm the main gates. When Braca informs Scorpius that they've entered the building, Scorpius sends all available troops to stand guard outside the main chamber where Crichton is being held.

Outside the generator room, Zhaan injects Teurec with the takar serum, but he's unable to create flame before Scorpius arrives. Taking Zhaan and Stark captive, it seems for a moment that Scorpius has won, but the Sheyang turns his weapon on himself and explodes in an impressive ball of fire. The generator is destroyed. Stark and Zhaan leap to safety.

With the power out, D'Argo, Aeryn and Behkesh unleash themselves on a corridor packed with PK troops. Even though Aeryn's night vision goggles aren't working, she manages to inflict substantial damage.

In another corridor lit only by a living PK soldier-torch who everyone ignores despite his screams, Scorpius has managed to survive the inferno in the generator room. Braca informs him that the monitors are out. He demands backup power. He's also unable to raise Natira on his comm badge.

Back in the main chamber, Crichton is still trying to convince Natira to free him. He tells her that Scorpy is planning on killing her anyway and she finally agrees to go inside his head and ask the clone (brainworm) the truth. She appears on the dock at Sawyer's Lake and confronts Scorpius. The clone, meeting Natira for the first time, finds her beautiful and enticing. She can tell just by looking at him that she's as good as dead. He smiles and assures her that her death will be painless. Natira kneels over Crichton's paralyzed body and asks for safe passage on Moya.

By the time Aeryn, D'Argo and Bahkesh arrive in the main chamber, the three are gone. The chip in Crichton's head gives him messages too hard to resist and he becomes immobilized in the corridor with Scorpius' troops advancing. Braca discovers the intruders in the landing bay just as Zhaan and Stark call for pickup.

Aboard Moya, it seems there is a traitor in their midst. one of the Zenetian pirates, betrays the others by deploying the Flax so that both the transport pod and Moya are stuck and unable to save those on the planet.

In the depository, Scorpius finally catches up with Crichton. Akkor tries to shoot Crichton, but Rorg pushes him out of the way and is mortally injured. Before he dies, he makes D'Argo promise to go to Rorf and tell her of his death. Crichton, enraged, tries to kill Scorpius, but ends up killing Akkor in turn. Scorpius realizes that Natira has betrayed him. Natira tries to get Crichton to flee, but he's immobilized. As Scorpius advances, D'Argo and the others arrive. Aeryn pushes Crichton to the side of the corridor where he sits fighting the demons in his head while the battle rages around him.

Zhaan and Stark, waiting at the pickup point, are getting no response from the transport pod. But they do hear from someone else — Crais. Talyn destroys the Zenetian ship and the Flax collapses. The pirate left aboard Moya, still determined to get something out of this deal, says he'll take Moya. Chiana, furious, struggles with him. His weapon discharges and for a moment it's unclear who's taken the hit. But then the pirate falls away, dead.

When Crais contacts Aeryn, she instructs Zhaan and Stark to make their way to the waste vents where Rygel will pick them up. Aeryn cuts a hole in the wall and sends Bekhesh through. Just as Crichton agrees to give himself to Scorpius again, she punches him in the face and instructs D'Argo to carry him and follow Bekhesh into the heart of the depository. They'll hide out in the containers to shield themselves from the blast of Talyn's weapons.

Rygel guides the transport pod to the pickup point and rescues Zhaan and Stark. They get away before Talyn fires on the Depository, destroying the entire building.

After everything is finished and all are safely back aboard Moya, Rygel gloats about their wealth, but he is the only one who seems remotely excited about it. Bekhesh promises to deliver the proceeds of the profits to the families of their slain comrades, Rorf and Teurac.

Aboard Talyn, Aeryn thanks Crais for his help. Though she anticipates that Crais will take his "payment," he tells her that Talyn returned without his intercession or guidance. Then, he asks after Crichton.

In his quarters, Crichton is desperately trying to place a single chess piece on the board. When D'Argo brings Jothee to see him, Crichton begs D'Argo to kill him.

CRITIQUE:

As multiple-part story arcs go, this one falls directly between the excellent sequence of "Nerve," "The Hidden

Memory" and "Family Ties and the much less successful "Look at the Princess" trilogy from this season. "Liars, Guns and Money" was a fast-paced, action-packed trilogy of episodes and for U.S. viewers, a solid return after an extended hiatus.

There were many nice comic bits, especially in this last segment. Aeryn's deadpan responses to D'Argo's requests — especially when he tells her they must take out the device which looks like a Gatling gun -- are right on the money. The trouble she has with her nightvision eyepiece, Crichton calling Natira Flau Blucher (a reference to Young Frankenstein) and Rygel parading around with Durka's head are nice moments.

Additionally Crichton's rendition of "Daisy" was a nice homage to HAL in 2001: A Space Odyssey.

However, there are several questions that remain troubling. At one point, D'Argo says they'll simply storm the Depository. Later, in the pod, he says that they will wait for the power to go out before attacking the central chamber. Does he mean, simply, that they'll walk right through the main doors during Moya's diversion or that they'll wait for the power to go out before entering the building. While the subsequent scenes indicate that the former is the plan they choose, this was confusing.

How exactly does Crichton's paralysis work? Scorpius attaches the device to his head before he enters Crichton's mind, but then knifes Crichton while on the dock. Natira has to remove the knife in the mind-world before she can free Crichton. Can he not move after the knife is inserted or once the machine is powered up?

The convenient plot device of the Zenetian traitor really didn't work. The plan, on the whole, will net them a wealth much greater than an injured leviathan. Just how and when did Scorpius contact Logan? Why wouldn't Moya detect the communication? It seems there was some additional explaining that was left out of the final cut.

And the bit with Durka. Falling in with Zenetian

pirates? That seems oddball, even for Durka. He's such scary character and is killed off so quickly. One has to wonder what was in the writer's mind. Was the actor angling to leave the show? Who did he piss off to get such shoddy treatment? The head also seemed remarkably well-preserved on Rygel's pole. Did he have it treated with some kind of Hynerian process to keep the flesh from falling off the bone or drive everyone out of the room with the smell.

The largest problem with these episodes, however, is Stark. As noted in the critique of "With Friends Like These," no one can seem to decide what kind of a person he's supposed to be. At times, he seems completely insane as though the Aurora chair has destroyed his mind. Then he seems bent on taking revenge on Scorpius for killing so many of his people, a loyalty that has developed suddenly over the past two episodes. Sometimes he seems to want to have nothing to do with Moya and her crew, willing to betray them at a moment's notice. Other times, he and Zhaan seem like the perfect partners — concerned about each other's welfare and determined to survive to find each other again. He's a fascinating character with incredible gifts — but someone on the creative team needs to nail down his character profile and soon.

Overall, these episodes hang together primarily because they're action driven. They are choppy and at times it feels as though the creative team just shot miles and miles of footage without a script in hand. There is an unfortunate cobbled-together feeling that takes away from the show.

Here, it's all about big explosions and lots of running through corridors. Lighting, costumes and character all fall behind pyrotechnics and special effects. Farscape isn't really this kind of show, and honestly, it shouldn't try to be. It's better at telling the smaller stories than these giant shoot-em-ups. Additionally, the budget for creating this kind of wizardry should be saved for the

Creature Shop and not blown on some explosion that only makes the show seem like every other so-called action show that's on the air.

Finally, though, what needs to be addressed is the continual dipping into the same story well. This is not the first time Crichton has been rescued, nor, I expect, will it be the last. The problem with this is twofold. First, they've done it before. It was exciting the first time, but now it's old. Second, Crichton is a regular. They won't kill him off. So, we all know he'll be rescued. Let's remember that this show is supposed to be a series of stories about an average-Joe like anyone of us caught up in a universe he doesn't understand that is proving much more dangerous than he ever could have imagined.

Literature — in all its various genres — is rich with tales both well-known and fantastic and new. A good television show should be as refreshing and as exceptional as the best of literature. The show has talented writers and directors and actors. There is no excuse for shortchanging the viewers. In essence, we are the ones who have put money into this show and have made it the phenomenal success that it is. And we deserve to see the very best of what the creative team has to offer.

As a writer, I understand the difficulties of writing on deadline, whether it's a book like this one or a work of fiction. One could argue that television is like anything else — there are going to be some scripts that look great on the page but simply don't translate. There are going to be times that problems arise and the final product isn't what everyone had hoped it would be.

However, the danger of success is that it can result in sloppiness — an attitude that assumes the audience is no longer critical of the product but willing to accept whatever little bones thrown us because we're hooked on the show. This is not true. And poor stories can lead not only to a loss of viewers but also to cancellation, despite the hype maintained on the Dominion boards on a daily basis.

So it is both with trepidation and eagerness that we look to the final episode of Season 2.

Grade: C
Grade for Trilogy: B

Episode 20221: Die, Me, Dichotomy

Location: On the Diagnosan's world and aboard Moya in the Uncharted Territories
Guest Cast:
Lani Tupu as Crais
Wayne Pygram as Scorpius
Paul Goddard as Stark
David Franklin as Lt. Braca
Matt Newton as Jothee
Hugh Keays-Byrne as Grunchlk
Thomas Holesgrove as Diagnosan Tocot
Writer: David Kemper
Director: Rowan Woods

SYNOPSIS:

Crais and Talyn locate a Diagnosan named Tocot, part of a race of healers who may be able to help Moya. Rygel finds Zhaan mourning on one of Moya's damaged deck. He offers her some of the spoils from the Depository and she berates him until he tells her that the crew has decided to keep only a few items and donate the rest for Moya's healing.

In John's quarters, Crichton bloodies his hand punching out Scorpius' image in the mirror. Aeryn tells him they've reached a surgical center that may well be able to remove his chip. She tells him to fight against the images in his mind. Finally, he looks into the mirror, and in a voice that sounds frighteningly like Scorpius, admits he is the only one there. His reflection shows John Crichton in

Scorpius' mask with a face remarkably like his nemesis.

Down on the icy and snow-covered planet, D'Argo and Chiana meet with Tocot and his negotiator, Grunchlk. At first the cost is twelve thousand credits, but as the negotiation process continues, the price increases to twenty thousand. They agree to pay it. When Chiana approaches the healer, asking about his complex mask. Grunchlk explains that even the smallest bacteria inhaled through nose and mouth at the same time would kill the Diagnosan.

Aboard Moya, D'Argo tells Jothee they have the credits to have his tenkas restored. Jothee resists. D'Argo deduces that Jothee mutilated himself during his captivity. Hurt and feeling terribly guilty about the suffering Jothee has endured, D'Argo snaps angrily at Chiana when she approaches him. She says she's trying to maintain a relationship with him and understands, probably more than anyone aboard Moya, how precious Jothee is to him. But D'Argo is clearly preoccupied and Chiana slips away when he turns to answer a question posed by Stark.

Enlisted to help Stark spread a numbing gas which will help Moya's healing, D'Argo and Stark soon find themselves giddy and silly as they are also affected by the gas.

In Moya's Neural Cluster, Aeryn finds Crichton tinkering. Although he says he's trying to eavesdrop on Crais' transmissions, she is suspicious. She tells him that altering a communication signal outside Pilot's control is not acceptable. The audience can see that Crichton has somehow metamorphosed into a Scorpius/Crichton hybrid, but all Aeryn can see is John. They share a poignant moment. But it's really Scorpius who is manipulating Crichton's mind. After they exchange words of love, he knocks her out. Then, in true Scorpius fashion, licks her face.

Aboard Talyn, Crias and Talyn are talking. Crais

says that Aeryn cannot be blackmailed or enticed. They agree that if Aeryn chooses to join them freely, they will tell her "the truth," but before they can finish their conversation, Talyn detects a signal coming from Moya. Pilot has also detected the signal, which is known only to Captain's rank and above. Jothee, in the corridor with D'Argo when he hears the news, wants to know why Crichton is using that frequency if he's never been a Peacekeeper, and more importantly, what Jothee's role will be in the upcoming adventure. But D'Argo cuts him off, saying it's too dangerous. Jothee protests. D'Argo shouts at him and walks away.

Jothee enters the Neural Cluster and sees Aeryn lying on the floor. Quickly taking in the situation, Jothee commands Crichton to stop but Crichton just laughs at him. Jothee then tries to stop Crichton with a classic Luxan tongue-lashing, but Crichton grabs his tongue, pulls Jothee toward him and punches him in the face, knocking him out. D'Argo, however, coming upon the scene, proves a more formidable adversary and renders Crichton unconscious.

Crichton is transported down to the planet. Strapped to a table, Crichton wakes to find Stark standing over him. He tells Crichton that the doctor is just going to have a look at what's going on inside Crichton's head. Crais arrives at this point and informs Crichton that both Aeryn and Jothee will recover. In a completely sterile environment the healer examines Crichton's brain by using a device that makes his skull transparent. When Crichton's skull becomes transparent, it becomes apparent that the infestation from the neural chip is much worse than anyone could have imagined. His brain is literally crawling with nasty black worm-like creatures. Everyone is horrified. Worse, the healer tells Crichton through his interpreter, Grunchlk, that there's nothing he can do. The effects of the chip cannot be neutralized without killing Crichton.

Awake and on his feet once more, Crichton is with

Aeryn at the entryway to a huge depository. Within the cavernous room are stored thousands of bodies, all frozen a moment before their deaths. Grunchlk claims they were all accident victims, but one wonders if the healer has other motives. Zhaan is incensed. She believes that both the healer and his assistant have interfered with the natural process of life and death. But Grunchlk is unapologetic. He tells Crichton he has three life forms, Interons, who have organs to donate to Crichton's cause. Crichton wants the chip out. Grunchlk is only too happy to oblige. There's only one catch — if the procedure doesn't work, they get to keep Crichton's body.

Keeping Pilot company as the numbing gas takes effect, Jothee tells Chiana that D'Argo has talked about buying a farm to grow prasa fruit and make wine. D'Argo, Jothee says, wants to live quietly. But that's not what Jothee wants at all. Chiana is taken aback. D'Argo, it seems, had not mentioned anything about a farm to her. As Pilot succumbs to the numbing gas, he becomes silly and accidentally shows them a tape D'Argo had made in which he asks Chiana to be his wife.

Rygel, meanwhile, has sought out Grunchlk. In true negotiator's fashion, Rygel rolls out a series of three small stones in an attempt to book passage, presumably back to Hyneria. The offering of a fourth, and much larger stone, is accepted.

Aboard Moya, Crichton has again been restrained to protect the others from the Scorpius within. Zhaan is tending him. Thinking he's going to die, Crichton asks Zhaan to share Unity with him so that she can relay the many messages he wants to send to family and friends. She agrees, only to discover that John is not in control. The Scorpius within tells Zhaan that it's a pity she's only a tenth level Pa'u if she had advanced to the twelfth level, she would be able to break his psychic hold on her. The result of Unity is devastating to Zhaan, and Crichton/Scorpius escapes.

Crais approaches Aeryn about joining him and Talyn. He talks about how different their childhoods have been: Crais was conscripted (or more appropriately stolen) to join the PK legion having known the compassion of a family; Aeryn was born and raised aboard a PK vessel in space. Talyn, Crais continues, has asked Aeryn to join them -- has chosen her to help guide him, and by extension, Crais.

Aeryn considers his offer and Crais leans forward to kiss her. They are interrupted when Talyn breaks in to tell them Crichton/Scorpius has escaped, is in the Farscape 1 and is broadcasting their location to Scorpius. Before she departs to chase after Crichton/Scorpius, Aeryn thanks Crais for his offer.

Although Aeryn is an exceptional pilot, Crichton/ Scorpius points out that she was not trained to fly in the resistance atmosphere provides. Crichton/Scorpius, on the other hand, spent most of his flying career coping with the restrictions of atmospheric gravity and quickly out-maneuvers her.

While Crais and Talyn try to scramble the outgoing transmission, Zhaan comes to consciousness with Stark at her side. She says that the Crichton they know is dead and his body houses some terrible evil.

Crichton comes upon Aeryn again. He's flying the Farscape 1 directly above Aeryn's prowler and when she tells him to land immediately, he deploys his landing gear right into her cockpit. She is able to eject before the prowler crashes, but her harness won't release. Crichton is able to regain control of himself long enough to tell her she has to get out of the chair. But it's too late. The ejection seat with Aeryn in it crashes into a frozen lake and the Peacekeeper drowns.

Inside the facility, Aeryn's body is encased in a cryochamber/coffin. Each member of the crew either say something or leave an object in her coffin (D'Argo gives her his qualta blade, Rygel his regency seal) while Zhaan delivers a moving eulogy. Crichton asks for D'Argo's knife and cuts a lock of her hair. Then he's led away in handcuffs to the operating theater.

Before Grunchlk departs, he tells Crichton that since they don't have a map of a human brain, Crichton will have to help the healer discern which parts of his brain control which functions and where certain memories are stored. As Tocot begins to remove the chip's tendrils bits of Crichton's brain come off with it and the healer activates various memories: Crichton's dogs, his relationship with Aeryn, American history and politics. Because the neural chip is located so close to Crichton's language center, the healer isn't sure he can remove the chip without destroying Crichton's ability to speak. Crichton tells him to do whatever is necessary.

Aboard Talyn, Crais mourns for Aeryn. In his hand he holds a chip. On that chip is information which would have made Aeryn extremely happy, he says.

In Pilot's chamber, Zhaan comforts Pilot while Stark looks on. After a moment, he asks her what she plans to do next. When she tells him her only concern now is for the welfare of Moya and Pilot, he tells her that he would be most honored to stay and be her companion and she accepts.

Meanwhile, Jothee tells Chiana he's never stayed in one place long enough to make any lasting connections; Chiana tells him she always stays too long. They lean toward each other for a kiss but are interrupted by D'Argo. He wants to discuss the future.

Down on the planet, Grunchlk informs Rygel that his ship will be arriving shortly. In the operating theatre, just as the healer gets the chip out of Crichton's brain and is about to start the process of replacing Crichton's brain, Scorpius and his troops arrive at the compound. Scorpius enters the operating theater and exposes the healer to contaminants, killing him almost instantly. Crichton, unable to speak coherently, is furious. Scorpius takes the neural chip and its tendrils, leaving Crichton strapped to the table.

CRITIQUE:

What a season finale! This one is a stronger final episode than last year's "Family Ties." In "Family Ties," it seemed logical that Crichton and D'Argo would eventually be rescued by Aeryn and then reunited with the others during the early part of Season 2. Here, however, there are many loose ends that provide many different possibilities for resolution.

The most shocking revelation is Aeryn's death. Although many of the crew members and other regular characters have come close to death before, this sequence was riveting. What works here is the quick cutting back and forth between Aeryn and the other crew members. Watching her face as she struggles with the harness and her friends' faces as they listen to the exchange between Crichton, Crichton/Scorpius, Crais and Aeryn really plays up the emotional connections that have evolved among these characters.

It also is great fodder for the rumor mill. Within a week, scifi.com had uploaded a fairly extensive tribute page to Aeryn Sun complete with the text of Zhaan's eulogy, a slideshow, downloadable clips of Aeryn's death (which I found borderline questionable -- why would anyone want to watch someone plunge to her death over and over again?) and a downloadable sound file of the funeral song, which was quite beautiful. Gus Gross, the man behind all the Farscape music has provided a haunting soundtrack for this moment. Kudos also to singer Elizabeth Campbell for her performance. My only quibble with the funeral sequence was the use of the word "Amen." For Crichton to say it would have been one thing, but since the show has used a number of words specific to the Uncharted Territories, this didn't really work. It would have been more interesting for each character to say something in her or his own way to signify that kind of closure.

Although the translator microbes are only supposed

to stumble over words that have no clear translation, this hasn't been the case from the start. And while there is a lot to be said for creating a separate lexicon for any show, the creative team should take these kind of opportunities to expand the lexicon and therefore the culture, rather than using the lexicon just as a way to get around the censors.

I doubt, however, that Aeryn is truly dead. Why? First and foremost, killing Aeryn could quite possibly kill the show. A big part of what makes the show go is the relationship between Aeryn and Crichton and without the "love interest" the risk of the show losing its fan base is high.

Second, the interplay between Aeryn and the other characters is also essential. She, as much as any member of the ensemble, is crucial to the development of the other characters, especially Crais and Talyn. There's a lot more to that particular story line that bears exploring especially with the giant hint about some very important information lurking on the PK chip in Crais' possession.

Third, the way in which she died leaves the door open for her return. Remember the healer's huge creature depository? Organs available for harvesting are available, which means that the bodies have to be in some kind of suspended animation or cryofreeze to keep them from degenerating. Additionally, Zhaan finds the whole scenario abhorrent because she argues that not only are Grunsclk and Tocot interfering with the natural cycles of life and death, but she's also convinced that the spirits within those bodies are still present -- in other words, they're alive.

Additionally, it's not impossible to revive someone who has drowned, especially in very cold water, due to the effects of hypothermia on the body. No, I suspect we've yet to see the last of this Peacekeeper — and thank goodness!

What didn't work about the death sequence had to do with Crichton. When he regains control of himself for the short moments before Aeryn crashes through the ice, all he can say to her is that she has to get out of the chair. She knows. She's already figured out that the chair's weight is going to drag her down and it's not as though she isn't trying to get the harness to release. Crichton saying that he won't lose her in this way is a step in the right direction. Their last exchange should be as emotionally charged as possible, as frightening and horrific for them as it is for us. Even having him repeat something, "Please, no!" would have been better than what we got. On the plus side, however, Mr. Browder nailed Scorpius' vocal cadences. Both the accent and the rhythm were right on.

Another bit that raises eyebrows are the death gifts. One has to suppose that Rygel can still reclaim his position without the royal seal -- at least we have to hope so! But D'Argo leaving his qualta blade didn't work for me. Although he is an impulsive and emotional character, this blade has been in his family for generations. It is the mark of who he is and how he sees himself. Additionally, did he not consider that Jothee might want the blade at some later point? What will he have to give to Jothee that might make the boy feel some pride in his heritage? The boy was clearly interested in the blade and in the story behind it, though that moment was cut short. Giving it to Aeryn, while appropriate on some level, felt like the wrong choice.

In terms of the other characters and relationships, there are some predictable and some unexpected turns in this episode. I was not surprised by the sudden attraction between Jothee and Chiana. D'Argo's vision of Chiana often doesn't mesh with who she really is. He wants to settle down, especially now that he's reunited his family. In this way, he seems much older than thirty cycles (a teenage Luxan, so to speak). It makes sense for D'Argo — he's found a woman he's attracted to with whom the sex is fantastic. He has his son back. He has recently acquired wealth. His life up to this point has been about uncertainty, loss and fear. He wants to leave that part of his life behind and start again.

Unfortunately, neither Chiana nor Jothee want what he does. Chiana's desire to experience adventure has come into direct conflict with her feelings for D'Argo. And it's not even clear whether those feelings run as deep. While she struggles to connect with him, trying to be with him in the here and now, he pushes her away. D'Argo seems to be someone who isn't very good at balancing the demands of daily life with his own inner peace and this often results in fits of anger directed at the person who finally causes him to lose control. In some cases, it's Chiana. At times during this last episode, it was Jothee. Crichton certainly has not been spared the Luxan's blunt rage, either.

But while D'Argo's motivations are laudable, the results are not. Pushing Chiana away while practicing his proposal creates a dichotomy (hence one reading of the title) that is not easily resolved. Trying to protect Jothee as though he were a small boy instead of a young man can only bring about dissatisfaction and frustration on both parts.

What Chiana wants and what Jothee wants are too similar to ignore. She's been portrayed as a thief, as a woman who can take care of herself, and as someone who definitely does not want to be told what to do or how to do it. Jothee, like Chiana, is used to watching his own back and he'll also bristle at D'Argo's protection, mistaking it for restriction.

I wasn't pleased to see Chiana as interested in pursuing Jothee as he is in pursuing her. His motivations are clear: Get back at Dad, have sex, refuse to play by the rules (even if that will hurt the ones closest to you), see how much you can get away with. It's all pretty classic adolescent behavior. Chiana, however, should know better. It's one thing to flirt on a Budong carcass to get your crewmates something to eat; it's another to kiss your lover's son. I probably sound like a broken record here when I point out, once again, that Chiana has been chosen to embody the worst stereotypes about women. How old is Jothee again? The creative team is really blurring the lines here about his age, Chiana's and D'Argo's.

Stark seems to have returned to his old self — that is the self present before the three-part "Liars, Guns and Money." His concern about Zhaan seems genuine as do her feelings for him. He helps her recover from the Crichton/ Scorpius mind invasion. She trusts him. They each have gifts which the other crew members struggle to understand. They're a good match. Let's hope that Zhaan makes it a priority to use some of their credits to get him a change of clothes. And speaking of clothes, it's nice to see her wearing the accessories which accentuate her figure rather than the non-descript sack she was wearing at the beginning of Season 2.

Rygel's desire to return to Hyneria comes as no surprise. As we have learned, it is only his thirst for revenge which fuels him. He clearly has no deep loyalty to anyone on the crew or Moya and Pilot. His motivations have always been clear. It's too bad the others were so quick to judge him when his devious little mind is probably the sharpest of them all.

Rygel is a hard character to like. As with the rest of the ensemble members, he has his good and bad qualities, but there is more emphasis placed on his "bad" qualities because they come into conflict with the needs and desires of the rest of the crew. If everyone were out to make a few extra credits and damn anyone who gets in the way, he'd be the hero (and show's star) rather than the smarmy little worm.

Chiana and Rygel's relationship didn't get enough chance to develop. It seems that once the writers acknowledged the fact that the two of them would always get everyone in trouble by making the worst possible choices, they were dropped as a storyline. The potential collaboration which was explored in "Dream a Little

Dream" has not been revisited in any depth. There are a lot of stories here, ones both humorous and serious that are worth exploring. That is if Rygel returns to Moya in Season Three.

Throughout the series, Pilot has been an underdeveloped and underused character. One of the best episodes of Season 2, "The Way We Weren't" was a tantalizing glimpse into the makings of a leviathan/Peacekeeper hybrid as well as the culture from which Pilot had come. More stories about Pilot would be welcome. Exploring the time between the initial bonding and the first episode of Season 1 seems like a rich time to mine for ideas. Flashback episodes are so incredibly valuable, especially if placed correctly during the season, and have been really underused so far. Each of the prisoners has a fascinating story to tell — and their lives overlapped so intimately. Some will argue, of course, that Crichton will not then be the focus, but there are ways to integrate him into the storyline without losing the power of the past.

The same is true for Moya. How did her species evolve? When and how were the first pilots and leviathans joined? Did another species aid in the joining? Who were they? How is a pilot chosen? What is the culture like on these worlds? In terms of human development, how long have these other cultures been in existence? Again, there are many fascinating stories which could be interwoven into the forward movement of the current timeline.

Both the Crais/Talyn and Scorpius storylines have been advanced this season, though more time has been devoted to the latter. It's not unusual for the creative team of any show to decide to focus primarily on one storyline per season. While the first season seemed to be primarily about introducing the characters and setting the tone for the series, Season 2 has tied almost every episode to the Scorpius arc.

Despite the enormous amount of time devoted to Moya's pregnancy, Talyn has not figured heavily into this season's stories. The reasoning behind this is not clear, but there are several possibilities. First, viewer feedback showed a preference for the clear demarcation of hero and villain which the Crichton/Scorpius story provides. Two, the creative team had not yet decided how to resolve the Crais/Talyn story and so allowed it to be on the back burner, so to speak, for a while. Three, Crais did not prove as popular a character as Scorpius. Four, viewers didn't like Crichton competing with Crais for Aeryn's affections, even if only in his mind. Five, the creative team wanted to solidify the Crichton/Aeryn relationship before introducing the "temptation" of Crais' invitation. It's clear that Aeryn has great empathy for Talyn and wants to be connected to him. This desire might even override her desire to create something permanent with Crichton as it would be more in her innate nature to choose a work-related situation over a personal one. And so forth. And while the Scorpius story arc has been fascinating, a different balance of stories might have been interesting. There have been many times that Scorpius should have at least been injured and he simply walks away unharmed. He can't be that infallible.

Crais, however, fares quite well in this finale. Asking Aeryn help guide the emotional being has a nice double meaning — it isn't just Talyn who needs help navigating the emotional seas, but Crais himself. His feelings for Aeryn are complicated. While it's clear he finds her attractive, what's not clear is whether or not he actually likes her as a person (or even loves her) or is simply interested in obtaining her help any way he can.

This final episode introduced — and destroyed — another interesting character, Tocot. That Crais should know of a race of healers was not surprising. He must have had some fascinating experiences in the Uncharted Territories since Talyn offered him the Hand of Friendship. It's possible that Crais knew of the Diagnosans' reputation from his contact with Scorpius. Imagine the rumor and speculation that might have gone on in any PK mess hall about a creature such as Scorpius.

Tocot's inability to communicate was problematic, however. While there's nothing wrong with allowing us to wonder about his ethics by having a frontman like Grunchlk to meet the new patients, his lack of language skills in the opening scenes compared with his conversation with Crichton during the surgery didn't work. First of all, it made Grunchlk seem unnecessary. Second, I found it hard to believe that Tocot would be able to make sense out of anything Crichton was saying given the language barrier — which reminds me, isn't everyone outfitted with translator microbes? How did Tocot manage to elude this most basic aspect of life in this part of then universe? What's frustrating about this is the problem is so easy to work around. When Grunchlk was introduced as the healer's negotiator, all the writers had to do was make it clear that Tocot was a healer, period. He doesn't want to think about the money aspect of this. He has left that in the hands of his "trusted" associate. This would also lessen the suspicion that Tocot was unethically dealing in slightly used body parts. Grunchlk seems the perfect business partner for Tocot — filthy where the healer is fastidious, greedy and generally unpleasant to look at and deal with. He's the proverbial secretary/gatekeeper you have to get past in order to talk to the boss.

So the second season ends with a great cliffhanger episode. All in all, this season has gifted us with a number of great stories, not just Farscape stories, but great stories on a universal level. As with any show, there have been some stumbles, but it is with great anticipation that I await the start of Season Three.

Grade: A-

Grade Point Average for Season 2: B

**Visit our webpage for additional Farsape titles
as well as novels, games, videos and more**

www.arabyfair.com